A Writer's

GUIDE TO

CHARACTERIZATION

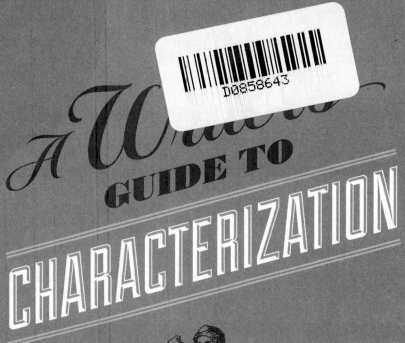

WRITER'S DIGEST BOOKS
Wr tersDigest.com
Cincinnati, Ohio

ARCHETYPES, HEROIC JOURNEYS, AND OTHER ELEMENTS OF DYNAMIC CHARACTER DEVELOPMENT

VICTORIA LYNN SCHMIDT

For more resources for writers, visit www.writersdigest.com/books.

To receive a free weekly e-mail newsletter delivering tips and updates
about writing and about Writer's Digest products, register directly at www.
writersdigest.com/enews.

15 14 13 12 5 4 3 2 1

Distributed in Canada by Fraser Direct
100 Armstrong Avenue
Georgetown, Ontario, Canada L7G 5S4
Tel: (905) 877-4411

Distributed in the U.K. and Europe by F&W Media International
Brunel House, Newton Abbot, Devon, TQ12 4PU, England
Tel: (+44) 1626-323200, Fax: (+44) 1626-323319
E-mail: postmaster@davidandcharles.co.uk

Distributed in Australia by Capricorn Link
P.O. Box 704, Windsor, NSW 2756 Australia
Tel: (02) 4577-3555

Edited by: Scott Francis
Cover design by: Jessica Boonstra

Interior design by: Josh Roflow
Page layout: Claudean Wheeler
Production coordinated by: Debbie Thomas

DEDICATION

To my family—Stephen, Sandra, Angela, Kimberly and Barbara—thanks for sharing your archetypes with me and for all of your encouragement.

ABOUT THE AUTHOR

 Victoria Lynn Schmidt (www.Victoria LynnSchmidt.com) is the author of *Advanced Writing Techniques*, *Book in a Month*, *Story Structure Architect* and *45 Master Characters*. She graduated from the film program at UCLA, holds a master's degree in writing from Loyola Marymount University, and holds a doctorate in psychology. She is recognized internationally as a journey and archetype guru for the creative writer and is now becoming known as the voice for the adventurous soul, offering journey maps for all areas of life. When her writing schedule allows it, she teaches at several universities.

TABLE OF CONTENTS

INTRODUCTION

"The moment you think you understand a great work of art, it's dead for you." —OSCAR WILDE

The main goal of this book is to show you how to add that special element to your writing that will make it stand out from the rest, and maybe even inspire readers to call it a classic. Most of you know how to plot and how to create a basic character. You may have written a book or two, but to be great at your craft you need tools and techniques that will conjure deeper meaning from your work. I hope this book helps you do that.

Why should you strive for more meaning in your work? Meaning, which is sometimes called message or theme, is what readers and audiences really want from a piece of writing, though they may not consciously acknowledge it. When readers sit down to give you their precious time, they are hoping to be uplifted, to learn, to grow, as well as to be entertained. Many of you have the entertainment part down, but now you need to go a bit deeper.

Meaning and message can be a very subjective thing. Your goal is not to impart the "correct" meaning/message/subtext/theme but to inspire your reader or audience to think deeply enough to contemplate it. You want to engage readers on that deeper level. It's up to them to see things in *their* own way, through the lens of their personal experience and desires.

> "Meanings are not determined by situations, but we determine ourselves by meanings we give our situations."
> —ALFRED ADLER

The first section of *A Writer's Guide to Characterization* covers many new ideas that I borrowed from Jungian thought and applied to the task of creating great characters. These ideas include the following:

- More Jungian typology to add a bit more layering to the archetypes
- Female archetypal interactions
- A questionnaire to help you select a female archetype
- Male archetypal interactions
- A questionnaire to help you select a male archetype
- Male and female archetypal interactions

Through the years I have met so many wonderful authors in the romance-writing genre, and I realized that none of these writers develop the romantic journeys in their books. So I set out to dissect the stories and to present the three main love plotlines one can follow in any genre of writing. Love concerns all people, and I believe writers can benefit by exploring it in the context of their art. So this book includes a section that delves into **The Three Romantic Journeys**.

I personally have studied many holistic areas of self-help and growth, and I have a deep affection for animals. Thanks to my studies, I found a whole new area of archetypes that I know will be of profound use to writers: that of the animal archetype. The lessons here will show you how your characters, viewed as animal archetypes, can create meaning and themes in your work. This book includes fifteen animal archetypal lessons.

A NOTE ON GENDER: I strive to alternate between the pronouns *he* and *she* for balance in the book. My use of a specific pronoun does not mean the information applies only to the gender mentioned. Both genders can cross over into any "type."

PERSONALITY TYPOLOGY

> "The least of things with meaning, is worth more in life than the greatest of things without it." —Carl Jung

While Jung is known primarily for his work on archetypes, he also developed a personality typology that sheds light on how humans approach life. This typology focuses on two types: Introverts and Extroverts. Within these two types each individual also uses one (or more) of four functions as a primary way of dealing with information and circumstances that come his or her way. The four functions are: sensing, thinking, intuiting, and feeling.

What follows is an overview of the four functions and how each one applies to writing and to individual archetypes.

Introversion or extroversion will act as the core of your character and determine how that character relates to the outside world and how other characters see him in this relating.

The functions will show you how your character is experiencing or taking in the information and circumstances of the plot as he faces them. They also help you make decisions on dialogue, clothing, mannerisms, style, and inner monologue, and thereby give you a solid framework from which to build well-rounded characters that are consistent. The functions offer another level to consider when using archetypes, though you can use them without archetypes if you want to.

Archetypes give you the deepest level of characterization, and these elements help you further focus and externalize archetypal qualities. In the best case, archetype comes first.

INTROVERSION AND EXTROVERSION

Introverts prefer the internal world of thoughts, feelings, fantasies, and dreams. Extroverts prefer the external world of things and people and activities.

FOR WRITERS: This means that a character that is extroverted will enjoy being around people and being outdoors. She will probably enjoy being

3

in the spotlight more than an introvert will and she will be much more willing to speak in public. This type of personality is suited to a character such as an actor, dancer, leader, or politician.

Knowing whether your character is an introvert or extrovert can help you when you are selecting scene locations as well. Will your character be comfortable in the library? Would she be able to keep her mouth shut there? Extroverts tend to talk a lot while introverts prefer to write.

When you think along these lines, your scene locations become less arbitrary. They can contain subtext and meaning, and therefore they enhance the characterization.

The functions

Whether a person is an introvert or extrovert, he must deal with the world. And each person has a preferred way of dealing with it—a way he is comfortable with and good at. Jung suggests four basic ways, or functions, of dealing:

The first is **sensing**. Sensing means getting information via the senses. A sensing person is good at looking and listening and generally getting to know the world. Jung called this one of the **irrational** functions, meaning that it involves perceiving rather than judging information. Tangible immediate experience is valued over discussing or analyzing experience.

FOR WRITERS: This means a character will use what he sees, hears, and notices to make a decision. This type of character will think a person who can't look him in the eye is lying.

> "I know he loves me because of the kind words he says to me (hearing) and the things he does for me (seeing)."

The second is **thinking**. Thinking means evaluating information or ideas logically. Jung called this a **rational** function, meaning that it involves decision making or judging, rather than simple intake of information. It's objective truth, impersonal analysis, and judgment.

FOR WRITERS: This means the character will process situations in the story by using logic, facts, and planning. Think of Spock in *Star Trek*. This type of character will likely think someone is lying because they either got the facts wrong or because they aren't making logical sense.

> "I know he loves me because we are good together (rational). We belong together and he must know that."

The third function is **intuiting**. Intuiting is a kind of perception that works outside of the usual conscious processes. It is **irrational** or perceptual, like sensing, but comes from the complex integration of large amounts of information, rather than simply seeing or hearing. Jung said it was like seeing around corners. It's all about possibilities and asking 'What could happen?'

FOR WRITERS: This means the character will make decisions based on gut instinct rather than logic. He will use his sixth sense, and he has ideas and creative solutions that will go against the norm. He will know if someone is lying because he "just knows it."

> "I know she loves me because I just know it (intuition)."

The fourth is **feeling**. Feeling, like thinking, is a matter of evaluating information. A character who relies on feeling weighs her overall, emotional response. Jung calls it **rational**, but not in the usual sense of the word. It is all about what value something has over logical examination of it.

FOR WRITERS: This means the character will evaluate the world through the use of her feelings. She may be empathic. She consults herself before acting. "Can I do this? Is this good for me?" She will know if someone is lying because she'll feel his nervousness.

> "He loves me because I feel his love when I'm with him."

One of these four functions is superior or dominates in each one of the archetypes, as you will see in the next two sections.

Among other things, such information can help you figure out what occupation each archetype is most suited for.

Each archetype is listed next with these elements mapped out for them, you can also look to my previous book, *45 Master Characters,* for in-depth information on each archetype.

PART 1

ARCHETYPES &
HOW THEY INTERACT

CHAPTER 1

FEMALE HEROES AND VILLAINS

THE SEDUCTIVE MUSE

- Loves to be the center of attention, is smart and creative, enjoys sex, loves her body and feels deeply. A good example is Cleopatra.

- As a villain, the Seductive Muse becomes the **Femme Fatale** who deliberately uses her charms to control men.

IS PHYSICALLY CENTERED

EXTRAVERTED: Loves external world and activities.

SENSATION: Receives information by means of the senses, great at looking and listening.

OCCUPATIONS: Artistic type—Poet, Novelist, Composer, Sculptor, Stage, Illustrator, Advertising, Inventor, Actress, Dancer, Healer.

BELIEF: *All acts of love and pleasure are sacred.*

THE AMAZON

- Loves nature and animals, values womanhood, is unafraid, willing to fight to the death, wants to be self-sufficient. A good example is Xena.

- As a villain, the Amazon becomes the **Gorgon**, who rages against injustices and is merciless.

IS PHYSICALLY CENTERED

EXTRAVERTED: Loves external world and activities.

INTUITIVE: Receives information through 'knowing,' a sixth sense.

FEELING: Evaluates situations according to her emotional response.

OCCUPATIONS: Realistic type—Craftwork is about her personal vision, Laborer, Activist, Anthropologist, Athletic Coach, Gardener, Teaches Young Adults, Security, Bounty Hunter, Solider, Store Owner, Rescuer, Nonprofit Organizations, Field Spy, Olympics.

BELIEF: *No one can make you feel inferior without your consent. Face your fears head on.*

THE FATHER'S DAUGHTER

Loves the city, prefers male friendships, will do anything for the team, confident and intellectual. A good example is Captain Kathryn Janeway in *Star Trek: Voyager*.

- As a villain, the Father's Daughter becomes the **Backstabber** who tramples others to reach her goals.

IS MENTALLY CENTERED

EXTRAVERTED: Loves external world and activities.

THINKING: Receives information rationally or logically.

SENSATION: Receives information by means of the senses, great at looking and listening.

OCCUPATIONS: Investigative type—May craft practical things only, Physicist, Chemist, Biologist, Mathematician, Editor, Broker, Manager, Research Scientist, Engineer, Teaches Adults, Private Investigator, CIA Agent, Intellectual Spy.

BELIEF: *Always expand your mind but speak your thoughts when the time is right.*

THE NURTURER

- Driven to help people—children, students or patients, is a great listener, generous. A good example is Carol Brady in *The Brady Bunch*.

- As a villain, the Nurturer becomes the **Overcontrolling Mother** who uses guilt and manipulation to manipulate others.

IS EMOTIONALLY CENTERED

EXTRAVERTED: Loves external world and activities.

FEELING: Evaluates situations via her emotional response.

OCCUPATIONS: Social—Psychologist, Counselor, Missionary, Teaches Children, Social Worker, Nurse, Recreation Therapist, Cook, Human Resources, Private Secretary, Volunteer Worker, Mother.

BELIEF: *With open hearts, women create the world.*

THE MATRIARCH

- Loves to be with family, enjoys entertaining, committed to her marriage, dreams about her wedding day. If she isn't married, she may run a business as if it were her family. A good example is Roseanne Conner in *Roseanne*.

- As a villain, the Matriarch becomes the **Scorned Woman** who is passive aggressive and needs to be in control.

IS PHYSICALLY CENTERED

EXTRAVERTED: Loves external world and activities.

SENSATION: Receives information by means of the senses, great at looking and listening.

FEELING: Evaluates situations via her emotional response.

OCCUPATIONS: Enterprising type—Leadership, Department Director/ President, Politician, Lawyer, Buyer, Judge, Mother, Professor, Banker, Architect, Company Owner, Principal, Sergeant.

BELIEF: *Always make time for your mate.*

THE MYSTIC

- Loves to be alone, tries to keep the peace, pays attention to details, spiritual, spacey. A good example is Phoebe Buffay in *Friends*.

- As a villain, the Mystic becomes the **Betrayer** who snaps and uses a fake persona to deceive others.

IS SPIRITUALLY CENTERED

INTROVERTED: Prefers internal world of thoughts, dreams and feelings.

FEELING: Evaluates situations via emotional response.

INTUITIVE: Receives information through 'knowing,' a sixth sense.

OCCUPATIONS: Artistic type(but introverted)—Poet, Novelist, Composer, Sculptor, Illustrator, Inventor, Gardner, Librarian, Day Care, Photographer, Nun, Priestess, Forest Ranger, Night Shift Worker, Psychic.

BELIEF: *Stop the chatter of your mind, listen to the silence and follow your own path.*

THE FEMALE MESSIAH

- Cares more for others than herself, strong belief system, inner strength and conviction that never dies. A good example is Joan of Arc. (Also, messiah characters can embody other archetypes.)

- As a villain, the Female Messiah becomes the **Destroyer,** who may hurt the few to save the many.

IS SPIRITUALLY CENTERED

INTROVERTED: Prefers internal world of thoughts, dreams, feelings.

INTUITIVE: Receives information through 'knowing,' a sixth sense.

OCCUPATIONS: Enterprising type(but Introverted)—Leader, Politician, Judge, Company Owner, Field Journalist, Activist, Police Woman, Run Spiritual Workshops, Social Critiques (like Gloria Steinem), Controversial Writer.

BELIEF: *One person alone can change the entire world, indeed that's all that ever has.*

THE MAIDEN

- Loves to play and go to parties, loves variety, sensitive, needs protection, may be close to her mother, adventurous. A good example is Lucy Ricardo in *I Love Lucy.*

- As a villain, the Maiden becomes the **Troubled Teen** who's self-centered, irresponsible and out of control.

IS EMOTIONALLY CENTERED

INTROVERTED: Prefer internal world of thoughts, dreams, feelings.

SENSATION: Receives information by means of the senses, great at looking and listening.

OCCUPATIONS: Conventional type—Cashier, Bookkeeper, Office Clerk, Assistant, Model, Actress, Fast Food, Flight Attendant, Sales, Waitress (especially nightclub), Bartender.

BELIEF: *Returning to my innocence feeds my soul.*

***

As you can see, the functions help further define the archetypes. You now know, for example, that an Amazon consults her *feelings* as well as her *intuition* when she makes a decision. So when she needs to take action, she will go with her gut regardless of what others think.

Of course her archetypal cares and fears may come into play, or even interfere—for instance, her feelings tell her danger is present but she must still come to the rescue.

> As she walked into the room, she could feel the tension in the air. Something was wrong. She knew it. She felt it. Why wasn't she listening to her feelings like she always did? Why didn't she run?
> The child, she thought, I have to rescue the child first.

On the other hand a Maiden will use her *senses* to make decisions. When picking a restaurant for her next meal, she will taste the food in her mind first. When deciding larger issues, she will listen to what others have to say before forming her own impressions and opinions.

> "Why can't she just make a decision like everyone else?" Daphne said to the salesman as she stared at Vanessa.
> Vanessa didn't pay her any mind, she wanted to pick the best couch she could find. After all, she'll be living with it every day. Especially now that she works at home.
> "This one is nice but, well, the cushions are a bit lumpy. That one's okay but the color is ... too ... bright. It just doesn't do it for me. Maybe I'll come back next week and see what you have then."
> Waving her hands in the air, Daphne stormed out of the store.

JOBS THAT GO AGAINST TYPE

It's not mandatory that an archetype hold one of the jobs specified in her category. In fact, if you mix and match the jobs, you can create a lot of comedy. This works well if your story is character driven, as much of the plot and subtext will be about her fitting in where she doesn't belong.

A good example is the film *Miss Congeniality* staring Sandra Bullock. She plays an FBI agent who is forced to join a beauty contest under cover. The writers placed their Amazon type heroine into a role typically suited for the Seductive Muse archetype and found many opportunities for comedy.

Once you understand what jobs are suited for each archetype you can then make better choices about your heroine's occupation and how it will fit into your story.

Maybe a Maiden has to work at a funeral parlor or a Mystic has to work at a strip club.

WHICH FEMALE ARCHETYPE SHOULD YOU CHOOSE?

Use the following questionnaire to help you figure out which archetype is most suited for your heroine (or for yourself for that matter). Doing so will help you decide which archetype fits your story idea best and push you to consider archetypes you may not have otherwise considered. You may find that some of them will drastically change your story direction for the better.

This quiz is inspired by one available at http://goddess-power.com/questions.htm

Answer each of the following ten questions for your character, rating each of the answers to that question, as it is true or not true for your character:

3 Strongly True/Agree

2 True/Agree

1 Almost True/Agree

-1 Not True/Disagree

Write the above score next to each lettered answer for every question. After you are finished (not before) you will find the corresponding letters for each answer to each question arranged underneath each of the Archetypes in columns. Simply enter the score you wrote next to its letter. I know this may sound confusing, but trust me, it will all make sense. Just take it one step at a time.

So for each question you will score EVERY possible answer. All of those answers have a corresponding letter in the answer chart that follows. Once you finish and view the chart, you should be able to figure this out. More instructions are found on the chart.

For example: Nurturer	Mystic	ETC.
1. B_	D	ETC
2. G_	E	ETC

This means that on question 1 of this made-up example, the answer that follows letter B applies to the Nurturer while the answer that follows letter D applies to the Mystic. If you scored a 3 for letter B and –1 for letter D that means your character is most likely a Nurturer. Since there are ten questions, you will add up all the scores that fall underneath the Nurturer's Column to get an overall score.

Granted your characters may have a high score in more than one column. This is perfectly fine—in life we are influenced by many archetypes—it's only in fiction and in film that one archetype dominates each character. As a result, the characters are more believable and consistent.

If your character scores high in more than one column, then you have an opportunity to make a choice about this character. Go back and look over the archetypes and decide which one you want to bring out more.

COMBINING ARCHETYPES: IS AN AMAZON ALWAYS AN AMAZON?

Essentially real people may have many archetypes within their personalities, but one usually dominates. When assessing a personality I ask 'What happened at an early age to cultivate this archetype in this character?' Usually an event that happened during the developmental years causes a person to adapt to survive, and the way she adapts shows her dominant archetype.

When people are subjected to stress, their dominant archetype takes over. A Nurturer can believe in independence and equality, but those beliefs don't make her an Amazon. Does she act to enforce these beliefs? Or are they only part of her backstory? In the major scenes, is she nurturing or speaking out? Basically we can all believe in saving the rainforest, but how many of us tie ourselves to a tree and fight for it like an Amazon would?

Likewise an Amazon, who raises children, let's say, doesn't cower when faced by the villain at the end of the story because at heart she's still an Amazon.

THE HEROINE QUESTIONNAIRE

1. WHAT IS THE MOST IMPORTANT THING IN HER LIFE?

a. Independence
b. Finding Herself
c. Fun
d. Marriage
e. Helping Others
f. Romance and Passion
g. Career
h. Goal

2. APPEARANCE—HOW SHE LOOKS.

a. She doesn't go out much so clothes and makeup aren't that important to her.
b. She prefers to be dressed in jeans and comfortable clothes.
c. Clothes are tools to get her job done.
d. She's often too busy helping others get dressed to think about it.
e. She loves to make herself look attractive.
f. Being well-dressed and made-up gives her the confidence she needs to go out into the world.
g. She likes to be well dressed in a conservative way and uses little makeup.
h. Her appearance is rather unconventional.

3. HOUSE AND HOME—WHAT MATTERS TO HER?
a. She prefers her home to be orderly and impressive.
b. She prefers the city; an apartment is fine.
c. Her home must be warm and have room for everyone.
d. She needs privacy and space for the things she likes to do.
e. She can live anywhere under any circumstances.
f. She prefers to live in the country or where she is close to parks and nature.
g. Wherever she lives must be comfortable and beautiful.
h. She needs lots of room to be wild or quiet in.

4. CHILDHOOD—HOW SHE USED TO BE (IF AN ADULT NOW).
a. She had lots of secret games and played in imaginary worlds.
b. She took a leadership role when playing games with her friends.
c. She mostly loved to play with dolls.
d. She always had her nose in a book.
e. She loved to be outdoors and with animals.
f. She loved changing clothes and playing dress up.
g. She engaged in solitary sports or hobbies.
h. She tried to develop her own games and invented her own language.

5. WHEN SHE HAS FREE TIME, HOW DOES SHE SPEND IT?
a. Cooking for family and friends.
b. Socializing with friends or attending a social events.
c. Doing volunteer work.
d. Shopping, especially for clothes.
e. Going to a bookstore, or reading.
f. Taking a walk/hike outdoors.
g. Meditating, quiet time or metaphysics.
h. Hanging out with friends, gossiping, risk taking.

6. LOVE AND MARRIAGE—WHAT DO THEY MEAN TO HER?
a. Marriage only works when there is a higher spiritual connection.
b. There is only one man for her: her soul mate.
c. Love is all-important; without it her marriage is empty.
d. Love and marriage are fine, so long as she has plenty of freedom.

   e. Marriage safeguards her children; love alone is not enough.

   f. Her marriage sometimes has to be sacrificed for the sake of her work.

   g. Marriage is not a luxury she can afford.

   h. Marriage is the foundation of society.

7. FRIENDS—WHAT IS THEIR PLACE IN HER LIFE?

   a. Most of her friends have children the same age as hers.

   b. She chooses friends carefully and they are very important to her.

   c. She enjoys discussing her ideas and work projects with both her women and men friends.

   d. She tends to have magical friendships.

   e. Her friends are mostly the wives of her husband's friends.

   f. She has very few close friends, but many acquaintances.

   g. Friends come and go in her life, jealousy is rampant.

   h. Her men friends are generally more important to her than her women friends.

8. WHICH OF THE FOLLOWING STATEMENTS IS MOST TRUE FOR HER?

   a. She takes care of her body so that she can exercise and be active.

   b. She struggles to make peace with her body.

   c. What she likes best about her body is its ability to bear children.

   d. She likes her body best when she knows her partner finds her atractive.

   e. She explores the limits of her body and mind.

   f. Her body makes her feel sexy and attractive.

   g. She doesn't spend much time thinking about her body.

   h. Her outward appearance matters less to her than how she feels on the inside.

9. BOOKS—WHAT DOES SHE MOSTLY HAVE LYING AROUND?

   a. Cookbooks, craft books, child-care books.

   b. Serious nonfiction, biographies, coffee table books, travel books, illustrated history.

   c. New age books, psychology, metaphysics, channeled books, I Ching, Tarot.

   d. Sports, fitness and yoga manuals, animal books, wildlife books, how-to books.

    e. Books on unusual hobbies and hidden mysteries.

    f. Alternative, independent, self-published books.

    g. Politics, sociology, recent intellectual books, avant-garde literature, feminist books.

    h. Art books, popular biographies, novels, romances, poetry.

10. THE LARGER WORLD—WHAT IS HER ATTITUDE TOWARD IT?

    a. She tries to stay informed about what's going on in the world.

    b. Politics only interest her for the intrigue behind the scenes.

    c. She knows more about the world from her dreams than from newspaper or TV.

    d. She knows what those in power are up to.

    e. It's mostly a man's world, so she leaves them to it.

    f. It's important for her to play an active role in the community.

    g. If it doesn't affect her family, she doesn't care to get involved.

    h. She rarely knows what's going on—or cares!

	Seductive Muse	Amazon	Father's Daughter	Nurturer	Matriarch	Mystic	Female Messiah	Maiden
1 =	F	A	G	E	D	B	H	C
2 =	E	B	F	D	G	A	C	H
3 =	G	F	B	C	A	D	E	H
4 =	F	E	D	C	B	G	H	A
5 =	D	F	E	A	B	G	C	H
6 =	C	D	F	H	E	A	G	B
7 =	G	C	H	A	E	B	F	D
8 =	F	A	B	C_	D	H	G	E
9 =	H	D	G	A	B	C	F	E
10 =	H	F	A	E	G	C	D	B
Totals								

On the above chart, you will find the ten questions listed from top to bottom. Enter your scores next to their corresponding letter for each question. When you are done, add up all the score for each column and record the totals. The highest scores show you which archetype dominates your character.

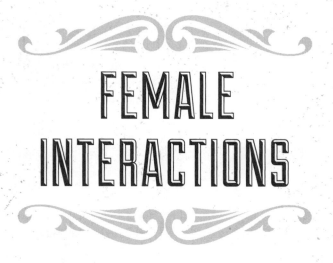

CHAPTER 2

FEMALE INTERACTIONS

In this chapter you will learn how all the female archetypes interact with each other. Not only will this information help you when you create supporting characters, it will also assist you in creating ensemble pieces (stories with two or more main characters who interact with each other). Supporting characters may have their own archetype, depending on how involved they are in the story.

Think of *The First Wives Club*, *The Big Chill*, and *Thelma and Louise* as ensemble story examples. They each have several main characters who take up almost equal story time. Each one of their problems moves the story forward.

Think of *Alien* and *The Wizard of* Oz as nonensemble story examples. They each have a main heroine (Ripley and Dorothy, respectively). Everyone else, except for the villain, is a supporting character.

In some cases you will notice that an ability or aspect of an archetype is so strong that no matter who you pair that character with, she will teach the same thing. That's okay. It just shows how strong an influence this aspect of her archetype is on the others.

The following pages show you how every female archetype interacts with every other female archetype. No matter how many main characters you have—you will be able to figure out how they mesh together.

Will you be writing an ensemble story, or will you have just one main heroine?

Here's where you'll start thinking about the other characters in your story.

CODE:

 = They will generally get along from the beginning.

 = They will generally clash from the beginning.

THE SEDUCTIVE MUSE AND THE AMAZON

PHYSICAL VS. PHYSICAL

This is an interesting pair—the Seductive Muse loves her body and is very spontaneous. She can go with the flow of life more easily than the Amazon who needs to be more in control. At the same time the Amazon is very accomplished because she can set limits and disciplines herself to get the job done.

They are both very earthy, creative, right brain types. Neither of them have aspirations to run a megacompany like the Father's Daughter. But, while the Seductive Muse will find a man to support her lifestyle, the Amazon will simply assume the lifestyle she wants and do what is necessary to keep it.

The Amazon can teach the Seductive Muse how to set limits and accept discipline as a positive part of life. She can teach her to be more selective in her choices and to value herself as a woman.

The Seductive Muse can teach the Amazon how to let loose and enjoy the spontaneous moments of life, how to be soft and sensual, how to pamper herself and enjoy the luxuries of life.

THE SEDUCTIVE MUSE
AND THE FATHER'S DAUGHTER

PHYSICAL VS. MENTAL

These two are opposites in every way. The Seductive Muse loves her body and is very spontaneous. She loves to be the center of attention and can be very emotional. She can go with the flow of life.

This is directly opposed to the Father's Daughter's way of life. She's in touch with her mind and does things by the book. She is all for the team and doesn't want to stand out as the center of attention. She can be very out of touch with her emotions and may see them as a weakness.

At the same time the Father's Daughter is very left-brained and smart. Top of her class and very accomplished. She can talk for hours about any intellectual subject and she knows her facts.

The Seductive Muse can teach the Father's Daughter to get in touch with her feelings and sensuality—her feminine side. The Father's Daughter can teach the Seductive Muse how to get along in the world and provide for herself in a left-brained, logical world.

 ## THE SEDUCTIVE MUSE AND THE NURTURER

PHYSICAL VS. EMOTIONAL

These two are somewhat alike in the way they are attuned to other people's feelings. They are both great at expressing love, but the Seductive Muse focuses more on romantic love and the Nurturer focuses more on unconditional love.

While the Seductive Muse *wants* men in her life to provide for her, the Nurturer *needs* someone in her life to take care of. This need makes the Nurturer somewhat of a slave to other people's demands. Being a slave to the demands of others is something the Seductive Muse, with her spontaneous lifestyle, can't deal with.

The Seductive Muse can teach the Nurturer to nurture herself for a change. She can encourage her to stand up to other people's demands.

The Nurturer can teach the Seductive Muse to care for someone other than herself and to realize the rewards of caring for and helping another even at great sacrifice to oneself.

THE SEDUCTIVE MUSE AND THE MATRIARCH

PHYSICAL VS. PHYSICAL

This is another opposing match. The Seductive Muse cannot handle all the planning, rules, and dictating that comes with the Matriarch. She needs to flow with life, not struggle against it or force it into a mold. Likewise the Matriarch cannot deal with how the Seductive Muse chooses to live her life. "Who will take care of her when she's old?" the Matriarch wonders.

The one thing they agree on is that a man should provide for the woman he's with. The way they "give back" to the man differs: The Matriarch raises a family and cares for the house, etc., while the Seductive Muse keeps herself beautiful and sensual. She's her man's fantasy. She knows she can (and is willing to) leave him at any time and that gives her power. The Matriarch will never leave her marriage. She finds power within her family unit.

The Seductive Muse can teach the Matriarch that control over life's events is only illusory. She can help the Matriarch through a crisis.

The Matriarch can teach the Seductive Muse how wonderful it is to have a family to rely on.

THE SEDUCTIVE MUSE AND THE MYSTIC

PHYSICAL VS. SPIRITUAL

The Seductive Muse loves to be out and about. Sitting still is not her cup of tea. The Mystic, on the other hand, loves to sit still and be alone with her thoughts. Put these two in a room together and the Mystic will find her patience tested by the Seductive Muse's many questions, movements, and curiosities—that is, the things she tries to entertain herself with.

Sometimes the Mystic chooses to be celibate, a decision the Seductive Muse will never understand. Sex is so fun and enjoyable to her. Why would anyone volunteer to give it up? (She could never pass up chocolate either.) Why deny yourself?

The Mystic is very into her spiritual or paranormal experiences so this may be one area for them to engage in conversation. To experience other 'dimensions' of thought is a right-brain creative function.

The Seductive Muse can teach the Mystic that sexuality can be a spiritual act in and of itself, that the self does not have to be denied in order to experience the spiritual. She can teach the Mystic to smell the roses and laugh it up.

The Mystic can teach the Seductive Muse to calm down and become self-aware. If the Seductive Muse has experienced something painful in her past and is trying to keep it hidden, doing so may be difficult. She doesn't want to analyze herself or her actions.

THE SEDUCTIVE MUSE AND THE FEMALE MESSIAH

PHYSICAL VS. SPIRITUAL

The Female Messiah gets along with everyone because she lives without judgment, but these two archetypes still clash. The Seductive Muse is earthy and the Female Messiah is otherworldly.

The Female Messiah is very self-aware and knows she is not in touch with her body. As she sees it, her life is not for her pleasure. She may live in joy and love, but she has a mission to complete. She is in the world but not of it and that is how she can see the truth of every situation. The Seductive Muse loves her body and enjoys the sensual side of life. Her mission is to be earthy, and she doesn't judge herself when she's around the Female Messiah at all.

The Female Messiah will always help those around her; that is, if they are open to being helped. It is unlikely that anyone will change her. She can show the Seductive Muse what it means to find true love inside oneself with the inner beloved. Full opening of the heart charka is bliss—and, unlike romantic love, you don't need anyone else involved in order to feel it.

THE SEDUCTIVE MUSE AND THE MAIDEN

PHYSICAL VS. EMOTIONAL

These two are very much alike. Both are somewhat childlike in their approach to life. They both love to play and party and be taken cared of. The Maiden is just more youthful and innocent. She hasn't been hurt as the Seductive Muse may have been, and she doesn't have the experience the Seductive Muse has either.

The Maiden can easily adapt. If she faces a hardship, her eyes will be opened and she will grow instead of becoming jaded like the Seductive Muse may. She also likes being dependent on others. She doesn't care about having the power to walk away; she doesn't want to walk away. She may want to find true love while the Seductive Muse has been there, done that, and moved on.

The Seductive Muse can teach the Maiden to see love for what it is without an idealized fantasy. She can teach the Maiden to accept reality and to watch out for herself in romantic entanglements.

The Maiden can teach the Seductive Muse to be more trustful and optimistic.

THE AMAZON AND THE FATHER'S DAUGHTER

PHYSICAL VS. MENTAL

Although these two are opposing archetypes in many ways, they both are very independent and self-sufficient, and they want to make it in a man's world as his equal. They are also both take-charge kind of gals who need to be in control.

While the Amazon values herself as a woman and doesn't care what men think about her, the Father's Daughter cares deeply what men think about her. She works day-to-day with men, trying to get up the corporate ladder. She plays with men and studies with men.

The Amazon can help the Father's Daughter get in touch with her female power. She can show the Father's Daughter that a woman can be whole unto herself. She can teach her to honor her cycles, something the Father's Daughter may want to suppress with pills.

The Father's Daughter can teach the Amazon that everything is not about gender. She can show her that men and women can get along and be great friends, and that there is value in fitting in and getting to the top as a woman.

 ## THE AMAZON AND THE NURTURER

PHYSICAL VS. EMOTIONAL

The Amazon understands how to nurture and care for others, but she doesn't understand why the Nurturer may lose her identity in the process. When she's around the Nurturer, she wants to protect her from those who would take advantage of her good nature.

The Nurturer knows she's not strong like the Amazon but she doesn't see the need to be. Her importance in the lives of all the people who need her help so desperately makes her strong. She contributes something and helps others just as the Amazon may contribute by saving the earth and calling others to stand up for their rights.

The Nurturer can teach the Amazon to stay focused and in one place long enough to do the right thing. The Nurturer won't give up on anyone, even if that person begs her to leave him alone.

The Amazon, on the other hand, will honor such a request and leave. Still, she recognizes that the Nurturer sticks with the problem and winds up helping the person.

 ## THE AMAZON AND THE MATRIARCH

PHYSICAL VS. PHYSICAL

These two types of women have strong opinions, which may be what makes them clash. The Amazon fights for all womankind and the Matriarch fights for her family.

The Matriarch finds her power through directing and supporting the lives of her family, friends, or employees. She is the rock, always there when others need her. At the same time, she expects everyone else to be there for her when she needs them. The Amazon is too independent for that. She will come and go as she pleases.

The Amazon can teach the Matriarch to value her womanliness and thus how to run things from a woman's perspective, rather than from the perspective her father may have taught her to run things.

The Matriarch can teach the Amazon how to organize a group and deal with people who look up to her.

THE AMAZON AND THE MYSTIC

PHYSICAL VS. SPIRITUAL

These two types are very much alike. The Amazon loves her solitude, though not as much as the Mystic does. The Amazon needs causes and people to fight for. She likes to be in the thick of things while the Mystic likes to be away from all attachments. 'Live and let live; everything will work out,' she says.

The Amazon can teach the Mystic how to take a stand and fight for what she believes in. The Mystic does have opinions and causes; she just supports them in solitary ways.

The Mystic can teach the Amazon to relax and take some time to renew herself. The Amazon's bones ache and her mind can get overwhelmed at times with all of her planning and fighting.

THE AMAZON AND THE FEMALE MESSIAH

PHYSICAL VS. SPIRITUAL

The Amazon understands having a cause or mission like the Female Messiah does. This is where they see eye to eye. The Amazon can't understand how the Female Messiah sometimes allows others to harm her instead of fighting back.

The Female Messiah can teach the Amazon to temper her emotions and to see the bigger picture. But this probably won't stop the Amazon from fighting back.

The Amazon can teach the Female Messiah to be careful not to get into a situation that forces her to make the decision whether to fight back or not to begin with.

THE AMAZON AND THE MAIDEN

PHYSICAL VS. EMOTIONAL

The Amazon and the Maiden make an amusing pair. The Amazon almost immediately feels responsible for the Maiden, and the Maiden is all too willing to let the Amazon provide for her. This doesn't mean the Maiden will easily accept the Amazon's meddling in her life or that the Amazon will be happy about having to provide for the Maiden.

The Amazon can teach the Maiden how to care for herself instead of relying on other people for her well-being. But this is a lesson that is hard to teach the Maiden.

The Maiden can teach the Amazon to accept help from others and to work well as a member of a team. The Maiden's free spirit may also rub off in small ways on the Amazon.

 ## THE FATHER'S DAUGHTER AND THE NURTURER

MENTAL VS. EMOTIONAL

These two women don't see eye to eye at all. The Father's Daughter will outwardly or subconsciously devalue the work that the Nurturer does. She wants to make it in a man's world, and nurturing is the first thing she must suppress in board meetings.

On the other hand the Nurturer may see the Father's Daughter as cold and unloving. She can't understand why she wants to go to the office every day. She enjoys caring for others. She may outwardly or subconsciously see her role as one that contributes more to society than anything the Father's Daughter will ever do.

The Nurturer can teach the Father's Daughter how to think about the people she's affecting with her work—for good or bad.

The Father's Daughter can teach the Nurturer that being smart and accomplished can sometimes lead to running a company—and that running a company can help more people than giving all your time to one person.

THE FATHER'S DAUGHTER AND THE MATRIARCH

MENTAL VS. PHYSICAL

These two women understand each other a little bit better. The Matriarch runs her family and friends as if she were running a company, a philosophy that the Father's Daughter can respect. Her boss may even be a Matriarch.

The Father's Daughter can teach the Matriarch how to play for the team instead of playing for herself and her wants.

The Matriarch can teach the Father's Daughter how nice it is to be the boss. She may inspire the Father's Daughter to achieve even more.

 ## THE FATHER'S DAUGHTER AND THE MYSTIC

MENTAL VS. SPIRITUAL

The Father's Daughter and the Mystic have one thing in common: They are both able to sit alone for hours. The difference is that the Mystic is usually enjoying herself while the Father's Daughter is looking for things to occupy her mind so she can get through the boredom.

Very often the Father's Daughter works so hard she doesn't know what to do when she has a day off. The Mystic can teach her to look inside herself to discover her true passion.

The Father's Daughter can teach the Mystic to come out of her shell. She can role model the joy of learning and reading about new things, and perhaps inspire the Mystic to go back to school.

 ## THE FATHER'S DAUGHTER AND THE FEMALE MESSIAH

MENTAL VS. SPIRITUAL

Of these two archetypes, we can make the stretch and say they both work on a team for the greater good of the 'mission,' but that is where the similarities end. In the end the Female Messiah usually has to go it alone when the rest of the team cannot follow through.

Many times the Female Messiah is trying to break apart the companies and systems the Father's Daughter holds dear. On an individual basis, the Female Messiah will (like the Mystic) guide the Father's Daughter to look inside of herself, a place she doesn't really want to go.

The Father's Daughter can teach the Female Messiah to think things through clearly before she acts, thus preventing a lot of mistakes that would force the rest of the Female Messiah's team to drop out.

THE FATHER'S DAUGHTER AND THE MAIDEN

MENTAL VS. EMOTIONAL

The Father's Daughter cannot understand a woman who can't or won't take care of herself. She may have had a difficult childhood, and when she's around the Maiden she is reminded of that time.

The Maiden can't understand a woman who would choose to be so strong, mental, serious, and responsible all of the time.

The Maiden can teach the Father's Daughter that it's healthy and enriching to let go and play once in a while, that life can be fun and enjoyable.

The Father's Daughter can teach the Maiden the value of a good education and how to plan for the future.

THE NURTURER AND THE MATRIARCH

EMOTIONAL VS. PHYSICAL

The Nurturer and the Matriarch both take care of others but the Nurturer isn't as in control as the Matriarch is. The Matriarch wonders why the Nurturer gives so much to those outside of her family.

The Nurturer doesn't understand why the Matriarch demands 'payment' for her services and expects people to act in a certain way. If the Nurturer is not careful in her relationship with the Matriarch, she will find herself under the Matriarch's control. The Matriarch can be very dominating, especially around someone who is so accommodating.

The Matriarch can teach the Nurturer to value her 'services' and to demand respect at the very least.

The Nurturer can teach the Matriarch that the people she helps already repay her in ways she can't begin to understand. They sometimes come back to help her because they are grateful, not because they owe her something.

THE NURTURER AND THE MYSTIC

EMOTIONAL VS. SPIRITUAL

Both of these gentle types come to the aid of others freely. The Nurturer, however, makes her life more open and accessible to them, and the Mystic guards her time wisely. They easily keep each other company for hours and make great roommates. The Nurturer can take care of everything if she wishes it, and the Mystic will not take advantage of her.

The Nurturer can teach the Mystic how to help others in a way that is comfortable to her. For instance, she might help those who are mystical and in need of guidance. The Nurturer can assure the Mystic that she need not be available to all for all kinds of problems and issues.

The Mystic can teach the Nurturer how to guard her time so she will have more energy to devote to her own work.

THE NURTURER AND THE FEMALE MESSIAH

EMOTIONAL VS. SPIRITUAL

These two archetypes may seem to have many similarities but in fact they are quite different. The Female Messiah will allow someone to be in pain if it is for that person's greater good and growth. The Nurturer can't watch a person suffer without trying to alleviate that suffering.

The Female Messiah can teach the Nurturer that perhaps she is giving too much because she seeks acceptance and self-esteem from those who need her. She can teach the Nurturer to look at the bigger picture.

The Nurturer can help the Female Messiah deal with people who want to cause her harm. Most people around the Nurturer 'owe' her for her help and would grant reprieve to the Female Messiah in her honor.

THE NURTURER AND THE MAIDEN

EMOTIONAL VS. EMOTIONAL

This relationship will have codependency written all over it, if the Nurturer and the Maiden are not careful. The Maiden loves to be taken care of and the Nurturer is only too happy to oblige. She may view the Maiden as the daughter she never had.

They can spend hours together at a time, neither judging the other for her choices in life. It's great for all Maidens to have a Nurturer in their life.

The Maiden has a natural gift of guiding others and the Nurturer can help her develop this gift. Simply seeing all the Nurturer does for others will influence the Maiden. She will learn respect for the healing arts and see compassion in action.

The Maiden can teach the Nurturer how to be more carefree and less worrisome, to trust the flow of life and live in the moment.

THE MATRIARCH AND THE MYSTIC

PHYSICAL VS. SPIRITUAL

These two archetypes make a bad match. The Mystic values her private time and will not stand for the Matriarch's demands on her. She may not voice her feelings but her actions will speak loud and clear, and drive the Matriarch crazy.

The Matriarch sees the Mystic's private time as selfish and inconsiderate of others. If the family is going out now, then she must come now. End of story.

The Matriarch can teach the Mystic what it means to be in a family—she can show her the rewards that are born from the drawbacks. It's a lesson in giving a little in order to receive. (For instance, the Mystic may have fun with the family even after she disputed having to adhere to the family's schedule.)

The Mystic can teach the Matriarch that everyone in the family is an individual and should be respected as such —that everyone has his or her own flow and timing to life. Perhaps the Matriarch would like to take a moment alone?

THE MATRIARCH AND THE FEMALE MESSIAH

PHYSICAL VS. SPIRITUAL

The Matriarch doesn't understand how the Female Messiah can pick up and leave when a cause or person beckons. The Matriarch's first 'mission' is her family unit and whatever problems and needs manifest therein.

The Female Messiah resists whatever guilt trips or manipulation the Matriarch may use in attempts to control her.

The Matriarch can help the Female Messiah if she needs someone to 'watch the troops' while she's off setting things up for them.

The Female Messiah can make the Matriarch aware that she is not the end-all of the universe, and she can teach the Matriarch that sometimes people have to be left to fall so they can also grow.

 ## THE MATRIARCH AND THE MAIDEN

PHYSICAL VS. EMOTIONAL

The Matriarch and Maiden pairing is not a good one for the Maiden. The Matriarch will not put up with her free lifestyle. If the Maiden stays home, the Matriarch will make sure she stays plenty busy. Perhaps she is jealous of the Maiden's free spirit and happy manner. The Matriarch has lost touch with her inner child, and she simply doesn't know how to be a friend to the Maiden.

The Maiden can teach the Matriarch to loosen up, but the teaching will take a lot of effort and the results may not last long. It may be easier for the Maiden to hide out for a while to get a break from all the stress and pressure the Matriarch brings with her.

The Matriarch can teach the Maiden responsibility. However, she may aggravate the Maiden to the point that the Maiden feels unsupported and goes to work just to get away from the Matriarch.

 ## THE MYSTIC AND THE FEMALE MESSIAH

SPIRITUAL VS. SPIRITUAL

These two archetypes can fair well if the Female Messiah is on a spiritual mission—but only if the Mystic is not jealous of the status bestowed upon the Female Messiah.

If the Female Messiah is on a political (or other) mission, the Mystic may lose interest and see it as a waste of time. She wants to stay clear of other people's drama or karma. It's all an illusion after all.

The Mystic can help the Female Messiah navigate the paranormal terrain, if her quest is spiritual, or the Mystic can help the Female Messiah hide out, if that is what she needs. The Mystic is highly skilled at evading others.

The Female Messiah can call into question all of the Mystic's beliefs, setting her on a roller-coaster ride of emotions.

THE MYSTIC AND THE MAIDEN

SPIRITUAL VS. EMOTIONAL

The Mystic and Maiden enjoy each other's company. The Mystic usually honors the Maiden's free spirit and sees a version of herself in her. The Maiden looks up to the Mystic—even if they are the same age—because the Mystic has more confidence and conviction.

The Mystic can teach the Maiden how to have something of her own at no cost. The mystical realms that she can dabble in when she has free time are there for the taking.

The Maiden can teach the Mystic that there is more to life than meditation. She can show the Mystic that life is full of wonder just as the spiritual world is.

THE FEMALE MESSIAH AND THE MAIDEN

SPIRITUAL VS. EMOTIONAL

These two archetypes don't clash but there's not much love between them either. The Female Messiah is not someone the Maiden can rely on. The Female Messiah won't have any vested interest in the Maiden one way or the other, an actuality which puzzles the Maiden, who is surrounded by people who try to befriend or control her.

The Maiden is put off by the Female Messiah's intensity. The Female Messiah is willing to take things all the way—to the death if she has to, and that is too much reality for the Maiden, who is less serious about things.

The Female Messiah can teach the Maiden to have a goal and see it through. She can show her that she is a spiritual being having a human experience, rather than a human being having a spiritual experience.

The Maiden can help the Female Messiah in many ways because she can move in and out of places without people taking much notice in her. They see her as just a 'harmless little girl.'

As you construct your scenes, you can use this information to bring out your character's deep inner world.

CHAPTER 3

MALE HEROES & VILLAINS

"Bond knew exactly where the switch was, and it was with one flow of motion that he stood on the threshold with the door full open, the light on and a gun in his hand. The safe, empty room sneered at him. He ignored the half-opened door of the bathroom and, after locking himself in, he turned up the bed-light and the mirror-light and threw on the settee beside the window. He then bent down and inspected one of his own black hairs which still lay undisturbed where he had left it before dinner, wedged into the drawer of the writing desk.

Next he examined a faint trace of talcum powder on the inner rim of the porcelain handle of the clothes cupboard. It appeared immaculate. He went into the bathroom, lifted the cover of the lavatory cistern and verified the level of the water against a small scratch on the copper-ball cock."—*Casino Royale* by Ian Fleming

While James Bond definitely has a bit of the Seducer in him, the Businessman archetype dominates. His identity as a spy is the most important thing in his life. He is a real workaholic and is very observant and analytical. The above passage illustrates this archetype by describing the way Bond approaches everything. He calmly checks all the traps he set for a potential intruder. He thought ahead and anticipated what the villain might do, drawing on his years of experience in the field. He sets several traps, not just one, and in different rooms. This is a man dedicated to his job. His deep inner world is that of a man who is suspicious yet professional.

This is an example of the kinds of traits that determine your character's archetype. While a character may display characteristics of more than one archetype, usually one will dominate. Let's examine the different archetypes for male characters.

THE BUSINESSMAN

- Has a strong will to get things done, thrives on order, loyal, trustworthy, loves work and being part of a team, very logical thinker. A good example is Frasier Crane in *Frasier*.

- As a villain, the Businessman becomes the **Traitor** who will do anything to bring order into his life.

Is Mentally Centered

EXTRAVERTED: Loves external world and activities.

THINKING: Receives information rationally or logically.

INTUITIVE: Receives information through 'knowing,' a sixth sense.

OCCUPATIONS: Investigative type—May craft practical things only, Physicist, Chemist, Biologist, Mathematician, Psychologist, Editor, Broker, Manager, Research Scientist, Engineer, Teaches Adults, Private Investigator, CIA Agent, Intellectual Spy.

MANTRA: *I am as solid as a rock, I am very decisive.*

THE PROTECTOR

- Is very physical, will fight to save others, enjoys travel, adventurous, in touch with his body. A good example is Rocky Balboa in *Rocky*.

- As a villain, the Protector becomes the **Gladiator** who is out for the lust of battle and blood.

Is Physically Centered

EXTRAVERTED: Loves external world and activities.

FEELING: Evaluates situations by his emotional response.

SENSATION: Receives information by means of the senses, great at looking and listening.

OCCUPATIONS: Realistic type—Craftwork is about his personal vision, Laborer, Activist, Anthropologist, Athletic Coach, Landscaper, Teaches Young Adults, Security, Bounty Hunter, Solider, Store Owner, Rescuer, Nonprofit Organizations, Field Spy.

MANTRA: *I am independent and care nothing about approval.*

THE RECLUSE

- Prefers to be left alone, rich inner life, sensitive, philosophical, reliable, is discerning. A good example is detective Philip Marlowe.

- As a villain, the Recluse becomes the **Warlock** who uses his knowledge to harm others. May hallucinate.

Is Spiritually Centered

INTROVERTED: Prefer internal world of thoughts, dreams, and feelings.

SENSATION: Receives information by means of the senses, great at looking and listening.

OCCUPATIONS: Artistic type(but introverted)—Poet, Novelist, Composer, Sculptor, Illustrator, Inventor, Gardener, Librarian, Animal Care, Photographer, Monk, Priest, Forest Ranger, Night Shift Worker, Psychic.

MANTRA: *Listen to the still quiet voice.*

THE FOOL

- Loves to play practical jokes, easygoing, charming, acts young, spontaneous. A good example is Cosmo Kramer in *Seinfeld*.

- As a villain, the Fool becomes the **Derelict** who cons others and hustles for cash.

Is Physically Centered

EXTRAVERTED: Loves external world and activities.

INTUITIVE: Receives information through 'knowing,' a sixth sense.

Thinking: Receives information rationally or logically.

OCCUPATIONS: Conventional type—Cashier, Bookkeeper, Office Clerk, Assistant, Model, Actor, Fast Food Worker, Flight Attendant, Sales, Waiter (especially at a nightclub), Bartender.

MANTRA: *Live in the present moment, forget the past, and dream of the future.*

THE WOMAN'S MAN

- Wants freedom above all else, is gentle, sensual, loves all women, has a sharp wit. A good example is Cary Grant in *An Affair to Remember*.

- As a villain, the Woman's Man becomes the **Seducer** who may act like a stalker.

Is Emotionally Centered

EXTRAVERTED: Loves external world and activities.

SENSATION: Receives information by means of the senses, great at looking and listening.

OCCUPATIONS: Artistic type—Poet, Novelist, Composer, Sculptor, Stage, Director, Illustrator, Advertising Sales Agent, Inventor, Actor, Dancer, Cook, Body Worker, Healer.

MANTRA: *Have fun, rejoice, and let go of self-imposed restrictions. Do what you will.*

THE MALE MESSIAH

- Questions authority, is disciplined, has inner strength, will sacrifice himself for the good of all, strong beliefs. A good example is Luke Skywalker in *Star Wars*. Messiah characters can embody other archetypes.

- As a villain, the Male Messiah becomes the **Punisher** who kills a man's spirit in order to transform that man.

Is Spiritually Centered

INTROVERTED: Prefers internal world of thoughts, dreams, and feelings.

INTUITIVE: Receives information through 'knowing,' a sixth sense.

OCCUPATIONS: Enterprising type (but Introverted)—Leader, Politician, Judge, Company Owner, Field Journalist, Activist, Policeman, Spiritual Workshop Leader, Presents Social Critiques (like Malcolm X), Controversial Writer.

MANTRA: *Stay focused on your goals, persevere, and you will be rewarded.*

THE ARTIST

- Loves to create and change things, instinctual, full of passion, intense, street-smart. A good example is Marlon Brando's character in *A Streetcar Named Desire*.

- As a villain, the Artist becomes the **Abuser** who's only out for revenge. He'll never let it go.

Is Emotionally Centered

EXTRAVERTED: Loves external world and activities.

CAN BE INTROVERTED: Prefers internal world of thoughts, dreams, and feelings.

FEELING: Evaluates situations by observing his emotional response.

OCCUPATIONS: Artistic and Social type—Poet, Novelist, Composer, Sculptor, Painter, Stage Director, Illustrator, Advertising Sales Agent, Inventor, Actor, Dancer, Counselor, Teacher, Social Worker, Recreation Therapist, Volunteer Worker, Activist.

MANTRA: *My work reflects what I feel inside, good or bad, tragic or magic.*

THE KING

- Needs family or group to rule over, forms alliances easily, loyal, giving, decisive, strong. A good example is Tony Soprano in *The Sopranos*.

- As a villain, the King becomes the **Dictator** whose need to control others becomes an obsession.

Is Mentally Centered

EXTRAVERTED: Loves external world and activities.

THINKING: Receives information rationally or logically.

SENSATION: Receives information by means of the senses, great at looking and listening.

OCCUPATIONS: Enterprising type—Leadership, Department President, Politician, Lawyer, Judge, Father, Professor, Banker, Architect, Company Owner, Principal, Sergeant.

MANTRA: *Speak your mind and hold steady when others are unstable.*

REMEMBER—JOBS THAT ARE AGAINST TYPE

It's not mandatory that an archetype hold one of the jobs specified in his category. In fact, if you mix and match the jobs, you create a potential for comedy. Watch the films *Mr. Mom* or *Kindergarten Cop* as examples of going against job type.

In *Mr. Mom* Michael Keaton is a man who stays home to care for the kids when his wife finds a job. *In Kindergarten Cop* Arnold Schwarzenneger plays a tough cop who is forced to teach kindergarten.

Once you understand what jobs are suited for each archetype you can then make better choices about your hero's occupation and how it will fit into your story.

THE HERO QUESTIONNAIRE

Use the following questionnaire to help you figure out which archetype is most suited for your hero (or for yourself for that matter).

Answer each of the following ten questions, rating each of the answers:

3 Strongly Agree

2 Agree

1 Almost Agree

-1 Disagree

See Female Quiz for detailed instructions.

1. WHAT IS THE MOST IMPORTANT THING IN HIS LIFE?

a. Being Right

b. Accomplishing Goals

c. Pursuing Dreams

d. Following Impulses

e. Work

f. Power

g. Having a Good Time

h. Analyzing People

2. HOW IS HIS TEMPERAMENT?

a. Unpredictable
b. Composed
c. Hot Blooded
d. Intense and Focused
e. Easygoing
f. Workaholic
g. Dominating
h. Emotional

3. HOUSE AND HOME—WHAT MATTERS TO HIM?

a. He prefers his home to be elegant and impressive.
b. He prefers the city; an apartment is fine.
c. His home must be comfortable and have room for everyone.
d. He needs privacy and space for the things he likes to do.
e. Wherever he lives must be 'inviting.'
f. He prefers to live in the country or where he is close to parks and open spaces.
g. He can live anywhere under any circumstances.
h. He needs lots of space to play around in.

4. CHILDHOOD—HOW HE USED TO BE (IF AN ADULT NOW)

a. He had lots of secret games and created imaginary worlds.
b. He always protected the weak ones when playing games.
c. He mostly loved to play with guns and G.I. Joe.
d. He always had his nose in a book.
e. He loved to be outdoors.
f. He loved acting and performing.
g. He played solitary sports and hobbies.
h. He tried to develop his own games and changed his name often.

5. WHEN HE HAS FREE TIME HOW DOES HE SPEND IT?

a. Drawing, writing, sculpting.
b. Socializing with friends or attending a social event.
c. Activism.

    d. Collecting 'toys.'

    e. Going to a bookstore or spending time reading.

    f. Taking a walk/hike outdoors.

    g. Working quietly, meditating.

    h. Playing 'manly' games—karate, shooting pool, hunting.

6. LOVE AND MARRIAGE—WHAT THEY MEAN TO HIM.

    a. Marriage only works with a woman who will let him have his 'alone' time. She can't be needy.

    b. Marriage is the foundation that allows him to work without worry of normal daily troubles. The wife does that.

    c. Love is all-important; without it his marriage is empty.

    d. Love and marriage are fine, so long as he has plenty of freedom.

    e. Marriage can give him stability but it can also be suffocating.

    f. Marriage is not a luxury he can afford.

    g. Marriage sometimes has to be sacrificed for the sake of his work.

    h. Passion is all important; without it his marriage is empty.

7. FRIENDS—THEIR PLACE IN HIS LIFE.

    a. Most of his friends have the same job he has.

    b. He chooses his friends carefully and they are very important to him.

    c. He enjoys exploring ideas and going on adventures with both women and men friends.

    d. He tends to have friendships with solitary people.

    e. His friends are mostly the acquaintances he meets with the same interests.

    f. His women friends are generally more important to him than his men friends.

    g. His friends are business associates he never really gets to know on an intimate level.

    h. He has very few close friends but many acquaintances.

8. WHICH OF THE FOLLOWING STATEMENTS IS MOST TRUE FOR HIM?

    a. I'm filled with creativity and spontaneity—I'm always up to something.

b. I keep to myself and spend much of my time at home.

c. I am most content and comfortable when I am working.

d. I like to be in charge and do things my way.

e. I love to party and I like to break the rules.

f. I am adventurous and often urge others to take risks too.

g. I am knowledgeable, I enjoy intellectual discussions and I like my world to be calm and orderly

h. I am very competitive and driven to succeed

9. BOOKS—WHAT HE MOSTLY HAS AROUND.

a. Art books, craft books, self-help books.

b. Serious nonfiction, biographies, coffee table books, travel books, illustrated history.

c. New age books, psychology, metaphysics, I Ching, Tarot.

d. Sports, fitness, and yoga manuals, animal books, wildlife books, how-to books.

e. Popular biographies, novels, poetry.

f. Politics, sociology, recent intellectual books, avant-garde literature, philosophy books.

g. Books on exotic places to make him look well traveled and smart.

h. Gag and joke books, fun stuff.

10. THE LARGER WORLD—HIS ATTITUDE TOWARD IT.

a. He tries to stay informed about what's going on in the world.

b. Politics only interests him for the intrigue behind the scenes.

c. He knows more about the world from his dreams than from newspaper or TV.

d. If it doesn't affect him or his company directly, he doesn't get involved.

e. It's mostly a corporate world, so he leaves the corporations to it.

f. It's important for him to play an active role in the community.

g. He knows what those in power are up to.

h. He rarely knows what's going on—or cares!

	Woman's Man	Protector	Business-Man	Artist	King	Recluse	Male Messiah	Fool
1 =	C	A	E	D	F	H	B	G
2 =	E	C	F	H	G	B	D	A
3 =	C	F	B	E	A	D	G	H
4 =	E	B	D	F	C	G	H	A
5 =	F	H	E	A	B	G	C	D
6 =	C	D	G	H	B	A	F	E
7 =	F	B	A	E	G	D	H	C
8 =	E	H	C	A	D	B	G	F
9 =	E	D	B	A	G	C	F	H
10 =	H	F	A	E	D	C	G	B
Totals								

On the above chart, you will find the ten questions listed from top to bottom. Enter your scores next to their corresponding letter for each question. When you are done, add up all the score for each column and record the totals. The highest scores show you which archetype dominates your character.

Example: If on **question 1** you scored answer **A** with a **2**, then go to question 1 above, find answer **A**, and place a **2** on the line next to **A**. You will see that answer **A** applies to the Protector archetype.

CHAPTER 4

MALE INTERACTIONS

In this section you will learn how the male archetypes interact with each other. Not only will this help when you create supporting characters, it will also assist when you create ensemble pieces. Supporting characters may have their own archetype, depending on how involved they are in the story.

In some cases you will notice that an ability or aspect of an archetype is so strong that no matter who he's paired with, he teaches the same thing. That's okay. It just shows how strong an influence this aspect of his archetype can be on the others.

The following pages show you how every male archetype interacts with every other male archetype. No matter how many main characters you have, you will be able to figure out how they fit together.

Understand that if your story is mainly about the plot and not the characters, you may want to go with archetypes that get along easily. Many cop buddy films feature two cops who are different in personality but similar in archetypes. They are both cops out to do the right thing and save the day.

THE BUSINESSMAN AND THE PROTECTOR

MENTAL VS. PHYSICAL

Although the Businessman and the Protector are opposing archetypes in many ways, they both are very independent and self-sufficient. They both need to be in control and take charge. The Businessman cares for the company and the Protector cares for people.

While the Protector lives in his body instead of his head, the Businessman lives in his head instead of his body. Career goals are not foremost in the Protector's mind but they are very important to the Businessman.

The Protector can teach the Businessman about taking risks and cultivating some adventure in his life. He might say, "Push yourself to see how far you can go." The Businessman can teach the Protector how to plan for the future, and thus avoid setbacks and complications.

 ## THE BUSINESSMAN AND THE RECLUSE

MENTAL VS. SPIRITUAL

The Businessman and the Recluse are very different, but they have one thing in common: They are both able to sit alone for hours. The difference is the Recluse is usually enjoying himself while the Businessman is looking for things to occupy his mind so he can get through the boredom. He doesn't have many friends outside of work.

Very often the Businessman works so hard he doesn't know what to do with himself when he has a day off. The Recluse can, reluctantly, teach him to look inside himself to find his true passion.

The Businessman can teach the Recluse to come out of his shell and teach him about the joy of learning and reading about new things.

 ## THE BUSINESSMAN AND THE FOOL

MENTAL VS. PHYSICAL

The Businessman cannot understand a man who can't or won't take care of himself. He may have had a difficult childhood, and when he's around the Fool he is reminded of that.

The Fool can't understand a man who would choose to be so strong, mental, serious, and responsible all of the time. He fights against the stereotype that men must be responsible breadwinners.

The Fool can teach the Businessman that it's healthy and enriching to let go and play once in a while, that life can be fun and enjoyable.

The Businessman can teach the Fool the value of a good education and how to plan for the future.

THE BUSINESSMAN AND THE WOMAN'S MAN

MENTAL VS. EMOTIONAL

These two archetypes are opposites in every way. The Woman's Man loves to be spontaneous and hates structure and rules. He can be very emotional. He is in touch with his body.

This is directly opposed to the Businessman and his way of life. He's in touch with his mind and does things by the book. He is all for the team and doesn't want to be the center of attention. He can be very out of touch with his emotions and may see the Woman's Man as weak and inefficient.

At the same time the Businessman is very left-brained and smart. He often solves the problems the Woman's Man creates.

The Woman's Man can teach the Businessman to get in touch with his feelings. The Businessman can teach the Woman's Man how to get along in the world and provide for himself in a left-brained, logical world.

THE BUSINESSMAN AND THE MALE MESSIAH

MENTAL VS. SPIRITUAL

Of these two archetypes, we can make the stretch and say they both work on a team for the greater good of the 'mission,' but that is where the similarities end. In the end the Male Messiah usually has to go it alone when the rest of the team cannot follow through.

Many times the Male Messiah is trying to break apart the companies and systems the Businessman holds dear. Or he is risking the entire goal of the Businessman to rescue someone. He can teach the Businessman that people and causes are more important than monetary success.

The Businessman can teach the Male Messiah to think things through clearly before he acts, thus preventing a lot of mistakes that would force the rest of his team to drop out.

THE BUSINESSMAN AND THE ARTIST

MENTAL VS. EMOTIONAL

These two archetypes don't see eye to eye at all. The Businessman will outwardly or subconsciously devalue the work the Artist does. He wants to make it in the logical world, and his creative/artistic side is the first thing he must suppress in order to achieve his goals. He can't waste time dreaming.

On the other hand the Artist may see the Businessman as cold and devoid of passion. He can't understand why he wants to go to the office every day. He enjoys creating and he may blame the Businessman for devising a society that devalues artistic accomplishments, thus keeping him from making a good living as an artist.

The Artist can teach the Businessman how to think 'outside the box,' to get creative with his solutions at work, and to value his passions if he can find them.

The Businessman can teach the Artist that logic, organization, and planning have valuable places in the world, for there would be chaos without them.

THE BUSINESSMAN AND THE KING

MENTAL VS. MENTAL

These two men understand each other. The King runs his businesses and/or family and friends using great organization and control, and that is something the Businessman respects. The King is more of a leader than the Businessman, who may be more of a follower.

The Businessman can teach the King how to play for the team instead of for himself.

The King can teach the Businessman how glorifying it is to be 'on top,' that is, as the boss. He may inspire the Businessman to achieve more, if doing so fits the Businessman's personality.

THE PROTECTOR AND THE RECLUSE

PHYSICAL VS. SPIRITUAL

The Protector and the Recluse are very much alike. The Protector wants to rule his own life and work hours. He wants his boss to leave him alone. The Protector needs causes and people to fight for. He likes to be in the thick of things. The Recluse simply likes to be separate from all attachments. 'Live and let live,' he says.

The Protector can teach the Recluse how to take a stand and how to fight for what he believes in. The Recluse does have opinions and causes, but he supports them in solitary ways.

The Recluse can teach the Protector to relax and take some time to renew herself. His body is sore from stress and fighting.

 ## THE PROTECTOR AND THE FOOL

PHYSICAL VS. PHYSICAL

The Protector and the Fool make an amusing pair. The Protector almost immediately feels responsible for the Fool, and the Fool is all too willing to let the Protector provide for him. This doesn't mean the Fool will easily accept the Protector meddling in his life or that the Protector will be happy about having to provide for the Fool.

The Protector can teach the Fool how to take care of himself instead of relying on other people for his well-being. This is a lesson that is hard to teach the Fool, who thinks he's fine just the way he is.

The Fool can teach the Protector to accept help from others and to work as a member of a team. His free spirit may also rub off in small ways on the Protector. He can also teach the Protector to walk away from a fight or to diffuse intense situations so the Protector won't have to fight.

 ## THE PROTECTOR AND THE WOMAN'S MAN

PHYSICAL VS. EMOTIONAL

This is an interesting pairing of archetypes. The Woman's Man loves women and is very spontaneous. He can go with the flow of life more easily than the Protector, who needs to be more in control. At the same time the Protector is very accomplished because he can set limits and he disciplines himself to get the job done.

They are both very earthy, external, right-brain types. Neither of them have aspirations to run a megacompany like the Businessman. But while the Woman's Man seeks women to fill the void in his life, the Protector would seeks other men like himself to wrestle or compete with.

The Protector can teach the Woman's Man how to set limits and accept discipline as a positive thing in life. He can teach the Woman's Man to be more self-reliant.

The Woman's Man can teach the Protector how to let loose and enjoy the spontaneous moments of life, how to be sensual, how to pamper himself and enjoy the luxuries of life. He can also teach the art of romancing a woman.

THE PROTECTOR AND THE MALE MESSIAH

PHYSICAL VS. SPIRITUAL

The Protector understands having a cause or mission like the Male Messiah has. This is where they see eye to eye. The Protector can't understand how the Male Messiah allows others to harm him instead of fighting back. Nonviolence is a foreign concept to the Protector.

The Male Messiah can teach the Protector to temper his emotions and to see the bigger picture, but doing so probably won't stop the Protector from fighting back.

The Protector can teach the Male Messiah to be careful to avoid situations that force him to make a decision to fight back or not to begin with.

THE PROTECTOR AND THE ARTIST

PHYSICAL VS. EMOTIONAL

The Protector is strong and fights for others, but he has control of his emotions to some degree. The Artist does not have control over his emotions. He can't seem to master them.

The Artist knows he's not strong like the Protector is, but he doesn't see the need to be unless the Protector is fighting against him. The Protector may even have to protect the Artist when the Artist insults others.

The Artist can teach the Protector to express his emotions and to look at the beauty in the world from an artist's perspective. The Protector can teach the Artist to take responsibility for his outbursts and to learn to control himself.

THE PROTECTOR AND THE KING

PHYSICAL VS. MENTAL

These archetypes represent two strong controlled men, which is why they clash. The Protector fights for others and the King fights for his family or his 'kingdom' in whatever form it takes.

The King finds his power in directing and controlling the lives of his family, friends, or employees. He is the rock, always there when others need him—but at a price. No one can refuse his requests. The Protector is too independent for that. He will come and go as he pleases. He will protect the King one day and fight against him the next.

The Protector can make the King aware of his broader responsibility to all people in need. He can show the King that he is in a position of power and should use it wisely.

The King can teach the Protector how to organize a group and take control of his life and aspirations. He can help the Protector network and build connections.

THE RECLUSE AND THE FOOL

SPIRITUAL VS. PHYSICAL

These two enjoy each other's company and can hang out for hours. The Recluse usually honors the Fool's free spirit and sees facets of himself in the Fool. The Fool looks up to the Recluse—even if they are the same age—because the Recluse has more confidence and conviction. He is able to stick to his guns and form his own life no matter what others think of it.

The Recluse can teach the Fool to be confident in his decisions and to welcome the responsibility of living on his own and on his own terms.

The Fool can remind the Recluse that there is more to life than meditation and that life is full of wonder, just as the spiritual world is.

THE RECLUSE AND THE WOMAN'S MAN

SPIRITUAL VS. EMOTIONAL

The Woman's Man loves to be out and about. The Recluse, on the other hand, loves to sit still and be alone. Put these two in a room together and the Recluse finds his tolerance for flighty people tested. He can't handle the Woman's Man curiosity and playful nature.

Sometimes the Recluse chooses to be celibate, and this is something the Woman's Man will never understand. Sex is so fun and enjoyable to him. Women are fun and enjoyable. He relates to them better than he does to men. Why deny yourself?

The Recluse highly values his spiritual or paranormal experiences, and this may be one area for them to engage in conversation since it is a right-brain creative function to experience other 'dimensions' of thought.

The Woman's Man can teach the Recluse that sexuality can be a spiritual act in and of itself and that the self does not have to be denied in order to be spiritual. "Live, love, and laugh" is his motto.

The Recluse can teach the Woman's Man to be by himself without feeling lonely.

THE RECLUSE AND THE MALE MESSIAH

SPIRITUAL VS. SPIRITUAL

These two archetypes get along well if the Male Messiah is on a spiritual mission and if the Recluse is not jealous of the status bestowed upon the Male Messiah.

The Recluse can help the Male Messiah navigate the paranormal terrain he is operating in if his quest is spiritual, or he can help the Male Messiah hide out if that is what the messiah needs. The Recluse is highly skilled at evading others.

The Male Messiah can call into question all of the Recluse's beliefs, setting him off balance.

THE RECLUSE AND THE ARTIST

SPIRITUAL VS. EMOTIONAL

These two solitary types are in touch with their emotions. Unlike the Recluse, however, the Artist handles being around people and may enjoy going out for a night on the town. He is very expressive compared to the Recluse.

The Artist can teach the Recluse how to help others who are mystical and in need of guidance. He can show the Recluse how to help in ways that are comfortable to him. He also can assure the recluse that he doesn't have to be available to all for all kinds of different problems and issues.

The Recluse can teach the Artist how to get in touch with his shadow side, or deep inner nature, to face his demons.

THE RECLUSE AND THE KING

SPIRITUAL VS. MENTAL

These two archetypes do not make a great match. The Recluse values his private time and will not stand for the King's demands on him. He may not voice his feelings, but his actions will speak loud and clear, and drive the King crazy.

The King sees the Recluse's private time as selfish and inconsiderate of others. If the King needs him now then he must come now. End of story.

The King can teach the Recluse what it means to be part of a group, how you have to give a little in order to receive.

The Recluse can teach the King that everyone in the family is an individual and should be respected as such—that everyone has their own flow and timing to life. Perhaps the King would like to take a moment alone?

THE FOOL AND THE WOMAN'S MAN

PHYSICAL VS. EMOTIONAL

These two men are very much alike. Both are somewhat childlike in their approach to life. They both love to play and party. The Fool is more youthful and innocent. He doesn't have the experience the Woman's Man has, and he doesn't know how to treat or deal with women either.

The Fool can easily adapt. If he faces a hardship his eyes will open, and he will grow instead of becoming jaded like the Woman's Man may. He may also fit into a traditional role if pushed toward it.

The Woman's Man can see life for what it is; that is, minus an idealized fantasy. He can teach the Fool how to see reality and how to deal with it while remaining playful and true to oneself.

The Fool can teach the Woman's Man to be more innocent and optimistic, and to simply get on with life when women leave him.

THE FOOL AND THE MALE MESSIAH

PHYSICAL VS. SPIRITUAL

These two archetypes don't clash but there's not much love between them either. The Male Messiah is not someone the Fool can rely on. The Male Messiah won't have any vested interest in the Fool one way or the other, an actuality that puzzles the Fool, who is surrounded by people who try to control or change him.

The Male Messiah can teach the Fool to have a goal and see it through, and also to see himself as a spiritual who is having a human experience rather than a human being who is having a spiritual experience. He will value the Fool's choices, knowing firsthand how hard it is to be different in this world.

The Fool can help the Male Messiah in many ways because he can move in and out of places without people taking much notice in him.

THE FOOL AND THE ARTIST

PHYSICAL VS. EMOTIONAL

The Fool and the Artist can potentially be two peas in a pod. The Fool loves to live outside of what is considered a 'normal' lifestyle, and the Artist is always available during the daytime.

The Fool possesses a natural gift for bringing joy to others. Simply being around the Fool makes the Artist feel young again. The Fool supports the Artist's view of life and validates his choices.

The Artist can teach the Fool to respect the arts. The Fool can share his views with the Artist, without worrying about being condemned.

THE FOOL AND THE KING

PHYSICAL VS. MENTAL

The King is not a good friend for the Fool. The King will not put up with the Fool's free lifestyle. If the Fool can't find a job, the King will make one up for him.

The Fool can teach the King to loosen up, but doing so will take much effort and probably will not produce lasting results. If the Fool needs a break from the King, his best bet will be to hide out.

The King can teach the Fool responsibility, but along the way he may aggravate the Fool so much and make him feel so misunderstood that the Fool wants to go to work just to get away.

THE WOMAN'S MAN AND THE MALE MESSIAH

EMOTIONAL VS. SPIRITUAL

While the Male Messiah gets along with everyone because he lives without judgment, these two archetypes still clash. The Woman's Man is earthy and the Male Messiah is otherworldly. He is also a fighter, while the Woman's Man is all lover.

The Male Messiah is very self-aware and knows he is not in touch with his body. His life is not for his own pleasure—he may live in joy but he has a mission to complete. He is in the world but not of it. The Woman's Man enjoys the senses of life and all of life's complexities, and would never think of giving them up.

The Male Messiah is always willing to help those around him; that is, if they can handle being helped. It is unlikely that anyone will change him. He can show the Woman's Man what it means to find romantic love inside oneself rather than looking to others to make him feel less alone and more fulfilled.

THE WOMAN'S MAN AND THE ARTIST

EMOTIONAL VS. EMOTIONAL

These two archetypes are similar in that they are both attuned to other people's feelings, and they are both practiced in expressing emotion. The Woman's Man is more focused on romantic love, however, and the Artist's interest is transcendental/artistic love.

While the Artist *wants* women in his life some of the time, the Woman's Man *needs* women in his life all of the time. This is something the Artist will never understand. He is attached to one project/painting at a time, and when it's finished he finds it easy to let it go. He sometimes wears his loneliness on his sleeve and uses it to fuel his art.

The Woman's Man can teach the Artist to play and to lighten up about his artistic endeavors. The Artist can teach the Woman's Man to create something of value and to see a project through to the end rather than leaving every time things get rough.

 ## THE WOMAN'S MAN AND THE KING

EMOTIONAL VS. MENTAL

This is another opposing match between two archetypes. The Woman's Man cannot handle all the planning, rule making, and dictating the King does. He needs to flow with life, not struggle against it. Likewise the King does not approve of how the Woman's Man chooses to live his life. He wonders why a man would have so many female friendships.

They agree that a man should have as many woman 'friends' as he wants; but the King sees these women as playthings and the Woman's Man deeply respects them as friends and lovers (unless he's a Seducer). The King will never leave his marriage, but the Woman's Man will move on as soon as the playfulness has gone out of the relationship.

The Woman's Man can teach the King that control over the events of life is only illusory. He can help him through a crisis.

The King can teach the Woman's Man to be more assertive and in control of his life.

THE MALE MESSIAH AND THE ARTIST

SPIRITUAL VS. EMOTIONAL

These archetypes are opposites, especially where emotions and drama are concerned. The Artist is all about drama and emotionality. The Male Messiah is detached from the drama of everyday life.

The Male Messiah can teach the Artist to look at the bigger picture when 'drama' comes into his life. so he can avoid the blame game. He can show the Artist how to be self-aware so that the Artist can recognize when he is becoming emotional before it happens.

The Artist can help the Male Messiah understand the emotions all the people around him are feeling, as well as the games they are playing.

THE MALE MESSIAH AND THE KING

SPIRITUAL VS. MENTAL

The King doesn't understand how the Male Messiah can pick up and leave when he feels 'called' upon to do so. His first 'mission,' and loyalty, is to his 'people.'

The King can help the Male Messiah if the Male Messiah needs someone to 'watch the troops' while he's off setting things up for them.

The Male Messiah can teach the King that he is not the end-all of the universe, that sometimes people have to be left alone so they can fall and thus grow.

THE ARTIST AND THE KING

EMOTIONAL VS. MENTAL

Both of these archetypes are very independent men. The King, however, is more in control of his emotions and has a clear sense of direction in life. The King sees all the creative work the Artist does but doesn't understand why he does it. His attitude is, 'What's the point?'

CHAPTER 5

ROMANTIC RELATIONSHIPS

Why are romantic relationships important?

If you want to build a story that will touch readers on a personal yet universal level, you need to add the element of love. Everyone longs for love on some level, and the best films and novels deal with the subject in one way or another.

All great books, movies, and entertainment have some sort of romantic theme running through them. Sometimes it is unrequited love. Sometimes it is passionate yet tragic love. Love is universal. It is something everyone desires, regardless of what they may say.

Keep in mind that many writers know how to write about the longing for love or unrequited love—great literature is filled with it—but the task of writing characters who have found love is much more difficult.

- How do they express their love?
- Who falls in love first?

- How will their relationship affect the rest of the story?
- Does the heroine's love for another effect or change her?
- Will they be together in the end?

As an author, you have several decisions to make up front regarding sex and love in your story. You may decide they have no place whatsoever in your story and that is fine, not every story has to have them. But writing about love and sex is still a skill every writer needs to learn. They are basic human functions, and love is a desire all your readers deal with in their daily lives.

Even action films include love in the subtext. Perhaps your hero is in love with a woman who has died. Such a situation adds a lot to his backstory—think of the *Lethal Weapon* movies.

After all, how many Heroes on the Masculine journey get the girl in the end? Many!

For all you skeptics out there, take a look at the following two love letters written by Napoleon and King Henry, and you will see that even a great solider, leader, or King can fall in love and reveal something of his character at the same time…

Napoleon Bonaparte to The Empress Josephine (February 1796):

"My waking thoughts are all of you. Your portrait and the remembrance of last night's delirium have robbed my sense of repose. Sweet and Incomparable Josephine, what an extraordinary influence you have over my heart.

Are you vexed? Do I see you sad? Are you ill at ease? My soul is broken with grief and there is no rest for your lover…

But is there more for me' when, delivering ourselves up to the deep feelings which master me, I breathe out upon your lips, upon your heart, a flame which burns me up? Ah! it was this past night I realized that your portrait was not you.

You start at noon. I shall see you in three hours. Meanwhile, mio dolce amour, accept a thousand kisses, but give me none, for they fire my blood."

King Henry VIII to Lady Anne Boleyn:

"...No more to you at this present, mine own darling, for lack of time.

But I would that you were in my arms, or I in yours for I think it long since I kissed you.

Written after the killing of a heart, at eleven of the clock; purposing with God's grace, tomorrow, mighty timely, to kill another, by the hand which, I trust, shortly shall be yours. HENRY R."

MALE AND FEMALE INTERACTIONS

In the following section you will learn how all the male archetypes interact with all the female archetypes. Such information can be used to develop parent and opposite-sex child relationships, opposite-sex friendships, and romantic relationships.

More often than not some romantic tension will exist between the hero and heroine. This section will show you how to build this tension and also the sub or main plot line of their relationship.

Love is something everyone longs for. It is a driving force in every life. This is why most books and movies contain some form of romantic relationship, or at least tension, within them. The hero and heroine don't have to 'get together,' but the thoughts, feelings, and tension around their relationship will play out all the same.

Once you've decided upon your main hero and heroine, you can check to see how their archetypes will fit together. This will be your last chance to rethink your main characters before you move on to plotting your story.

There will be some repetition but when you use the interations you usually will be looking at only one or two of them. So instead of having to read them all to get the full picture I have repeated some of the facts.

CODE:

 = they will generally get along from the beginning.

 = they will generally clash from the beginning.

Here's where you'll start thinking about the romantic relationships in your story—unless you choose not to have one:

THE BUSINESSMAN AND THE SEDUCTIVE MUSE

MENTAL VS. PHYSICAL

SELF-ESTEEM motivates the Businessman, and SELF-ACTUALIZATION motivates the Seductive Muse. He needs to learn to let go of his inhibitions, something the Seductive Muse is very good at. She wants to be recognized for her brains, not just her looks, which is the Businessman's forte.

The Businessman has a hard time being around someone who is so in touch with his or her body—especially a woman.

He may feel like a shy, confused schoolboy when he's around her, and he may not know what to do with her. Or he may have had such an intense day at work that he enjoys the sensual stimulation she provides. He wants to give his mind a rest, and she is just the person for the job. But can he see her as a potential wife? Will she support his career?

She's not one to be the perfect stay-at-home wife. She may stay home but she's no June Cleaver. The Seductive Muse sees the Businessman as stable and comfortable. She enjoys pushing his physical buttons and seeing him challenge himself physically. He's so uncoordinated.

Or if he does not have the take-charge personality she craves, she may see him as a mere rube, someone she can manipulate and take advantage of.

THE BUSINESSMAN AND THE AMAZON

MENTAL VS. PHYSICAL

SELF-ESTEEM motivates the Businessman, and SURVIVAL motivates the Amazon. He needs to learn to let go of his inhibitions, and if they are doing physical activities—hang gliding and bungee jumping can really loosen him up—the Amazon can help him with that. She wants to find a place of her own and to be recognized for her contributions. The Businessman may not value the same things she does.

The Businessman may not know how to act around the Amazon. She may be tougher than he is and this may make him feel like less of a man. In turn, he may be short with her and uncooperative. He may use his brains to make her feel stupid. Or he may like the dominatrix type and seek her out.

She has a hard time understanding all the intellectual jargon he uses, and she wonders if he is trying to impress her or make her feel stupid. He can be a good balance for her if he's assertive, but if he's not, they will have a tough time making things work.

 THE BUSINESSMAN AND THE FATHER'S DAUGHTER

MENTAL VS. MENTAL

SELF-ESTEEM motivates the Businessman, and THE NEED TO KNOW AND UNDERSTAND motivates the Father's Daughter. He needs to learn to let go of his inhibitions, and so does the Father's Daughter. She needs to get back to nature and to value herself as a woman, two things the Businessman cannot help her with.

They are very comfortable around each other. They work in the same type of environment, they take their work home with them, they work long hours, and both have a hard time socializing with those outside of their business circle.

They may see each other as 'the perfect match,' but things could get boring with all the similarities between them, especially if they work in the same office. She gets along with the men in the office so well, he may get jealous. Instead of talking to her about his insecurities he will get antagonistic and push her away, afraid of getting hurt.

She likes being the only female in the group. If they go out with a group of co-workers after work, she prefers (if only subconsciously) that the other females are Father's Daughters too. Different archetypes can make her feel out of place. She doesn't know how to flirt.

THE BUSINESSMAN AND THE NURTURER

MENTAL VS. EMOTIONAL

SELF-ESTEEM motivates the Businessman, and LOVE AND BELONGING motivates the Nurturer. He needs to learn to let go of his inhibitions, and if he tells her this outright, she will try to help him with it. She tries to help in every situation, but he may not know what he needs.

The Nurturer needs to let go of her attachment to others and find her own identity. This is not something the Businessman can help her with. He may provide the home base for her to work from, but he won't want her to change. He wants his home to remain constant so he can focus on work.

He may exploit her need to help others by asking her to help people at work and to entertain his clients. He may feel a sense of pride about the work she does, and he may enjoy people at work talking about how wonderful she is. But he can't fully understand what it is like to put others ahead of oneself. He puts the company first, but only to ensure his career.

The Nurturer will be happy if the Businessman's job has something to do with helping others; for instance, if he works for a nonprofit organization or something similar. She may push his buttons if he's materialistic and unsympathetic with others. In her mind, he better put a quarter into the homeless person's paper cup when they walk down the city street, and he better be able to deal with her need to tend to others.

THE BUSINESSMAN AND THE MATRIARCH

MENTAL VS. PHYSICAL

SELF-ESTEEM motivates the Businessman, and LOVE, BELONGING, AND RESPECT motivate the Matriarch. He needs to learn to let go of his inhibitions, but he will not be able to do so in a life with the Matriarch— she loves to be in control and prefers him to be inhibited because then she can step up to the plate.

She needs to commit to herself as much as she commits her husband or family. With the Businessman she will concern herself with playing the perfect wife and entertaining his clients and co-workers in their home. She will take care of everything. In this way he may take her for granted, but not for long. If he doesn't realize his error soon enough, she will stand up for herself.

The Businessman may not respect the Matriarch's choice to become a homemaker because to him career is the most important thing and taking care of the home is not a career.

The Matriarch respects what he does, but she feels her job is much more important. She shapes the lives of her family, and as such she believes that he couldn't be where he is without her.

If they aren't married, these two characters will see each other as safe bets for a long-term relationship when they meet.

 ## THE BUSINESSMAN AND THE MYSTIC

MENTAL VS. SPIRITUAL

SELF-ESTEEM motivates the Businessman, and AESTHETIC NEED FOR BALANCE motivates the Mystic. He needs to learn to let go of his inhibitions, and this will not happen easily with the Mystic. She focuses on her own need for solitude and her spiritual pursuits.

She needs to learn to be assertive, to go out and experience life. If he's a strong man, he can teach her to be assertive, but he has a busy schedule and may not be able to motivate her to go out.

He may be in awe of her spiritual, paranormal abilities. They may offer a great escape from his day-to-day grind, and he will look forward to seeing her.

He probably won't believe in anything but science. For him, it must be proven to be real. This is where these two archetypes clash—he may even attack her core beliefs. On the other hand, she can't understand why he wants to sit in a stuffy office and may respect a construction worker more than a businessperson.

 ## THE BUSINESSMAN AND THE FEMALE MESSIAH

MENTAL VS. SPIRITUAL

SELF-ESTEEM motivates the Businessman, and an AESTHETIC NEED TO BE CONNECTED TO SOMETHING GREATER motivates the Female Messiah. He needs to learn to let go of his inhibitions, and she can help him with this, but he may not enjoy the way she goes about it. She can push people hard to change.

She needs to learn to let go of the outcome of events and to trust what guides her. He is so used to structure and planning that he can't help her with this at all. He's not even sure he believes what she believes. If he's willing to suspend his disbelief, he can be an asset by helping her plan things out.

If he refuses to take her seriously or believe in her, he will be a drawback. He may cause her to doubt herself and her task. He may also do too much analyzing for her taste.

In general, she won't sit still for too long unless she's living in an oppressive society for women. This kind of woman doesn't fit well with the Businessman, who finds a career and stays put for as long as it takes to accomplish his goals. She always has a new agenda or cause to work for.

THE BUSINESSMAN AND THE MAIDEN

MENTAL VS. EMOTIONAL

SELF-ESTEEM motivates the Businessman, and SAFETY AND SECURITY motivate the Maiden. He needs to learn to let go of his inhibitions; this is something the Maiden is great at. She is very spontaneous and adventurous at times, and knows how to draw him out of the office and into the world.

She needs to stand on her own two feet. While the Businessman may take care of her financially, he won't necessarily be there for her emotionally or physically. He will be working and, therefore, away from her. This will force her to stand on her own two feet. She will be alone most of the time and will have to figure out who she is and what her interests are.

The Businessman can feel young around the Maiden, and he enjoys showing her off to his friends and co-workers. 'See how much fun she is and how lively?' She will express all the emotions he holds back. This may allow him to stay in his mind and figure things out. If they both get emotional, nothing will get done, he rationalizes. In this way he seems like a rock to her. She will choose him for a mate unless she meets a Protector first.

The Businessman doesn't need or expect her to financially support him or their family, if they have one, so he's fine with whatever she wants to do with her day—and that is exactly what she wants in a man.

They clash if he refuses to let his guard down in an effort to have fun with her or if she refuses to allow him to talk on an intellectual level. He may want her to read books so they can talk about his interests, but she may have a hard time with that depending on the subject.

 ## THE PROTECTOR AND THE SEDUCTIVE MUSE

PHYSICAL VS. PHYSICAL

SURVIVAL motivates the Protector, and SELF-ACTUALIZATION motivates the Seductive Muse. He needs to learn self-control because he frequently flies off the handle, though not necessarily in a violent way. The Seductive Muse is also very physical and needs to learn self-control, so she's not a great candidate to teach the Protector. She wants to be recognized for her brains, not just her looks, but because the Protector is so physically oriented, he can't help but notice her looks.

The Protector loves to be around people who are in touch with their bodies, especially a woman. He loves sports, martial arts, and anything kinesthetic.

He may see the Seductive Muse as a wonderful playmate and confidant. He feels like she understands him and like they operate on the same wavelength, but not when she goes into creative mode. He doesn't pursue his creative side, though he might be good at creative ventures. Tapping into his creative side is too internal and mental for him. He's fun and outdoorsy. She's fun and outgoing.

She's not inclined to be the perfect stay-at-home wife. She may stay home, but she's no June Cleaver. The Seductive Muse sees the Protector as fun and adventurous, but a little too intense for her taste. She knows he is not one to commit to, but she will enjoy his company all the same. She loves a take-charge kind of guy, and he can definitely take charge, except when it comes to his emotions.

 ## THE PROTECTOR AND THE AMAZON

PHYSICAL VS. PHYSICAL

SURVIVAL motivates the Protector, and SURVIVAL motivates the Amazon. He needs to learn self-control because he frequently flies off the handle, though not necessarily in a violent way. This is not something the Amazon would put up with for long. She will not allow any man to talk to her in a harsh way. She wants to find a place of her own, and she wants to be recognized for her contributions. The Protector will value what she does because he's just like her, but that's also the problem—they are too much alike.

The Amazon doesn't want to be protected or saved; she wants to do that herself. The Protector wants to protect her and gets frustrated when she won't let him do his job. If she messes up even in the slightest, he will point it out to her with an 'I told you so' attitude.

He may not know how to act around the Amazon because he's used to having to protect most other people. When she accomplishes something he has done, he feels like he should do something bigger, better, and this attitude sets them off on a competitive tangent.

She has a hard time understanding why he feels the need to protect her, and she wonders why he doesn't see that she can care for herself. Maybe she needs to learn to work with others or accept their help?

THE PROTECTOR AND THE FATHER'S DAUGHTER

PHYSICAL VS. MENTAL

SURVIVAL motivates the Protector, and THE NEED TO KNOW AND UNDERSTAND motivates the Father's Daughter. He needs to learn self-control because he frequently flies off the handle, though not necessarily in a violent way. This may be something the Father's Daughter is used to—she has been around stressed businessmen in meetings, etc.—so she may not be much help in teaching self-control. But the Protector also needs to learn how to use his mind instead of his brawn, and this is something the Father's Daughter can help with.

She needs to learn to let go of her inhibitions, to get back to nature, and to value herself as a woman. The Protector can help her with her inhibitions, and he can get her back into nature, but he can't help her value herself as a woman. As he would say, 'women need to be protected.' This is not to say he doesn't respect and admire women.

As a couple, they are not very comfortable around each other. He has a hard time understanding the intellectual jargon she uses and wonders if she is she trying to impress him or make him feel stupid. She can be a good balance for him, but they will have a tough time making things work if she's too assertive. She's attracted to powerful men, which he is, but he may not be mentally focused enough for her taste.

She likes being the only female in the group and feels she is the exception: "the Protector may need to protect other women but I can get along on my own."

THE PROTECTOR AND THE NURTURER

MENTAL VS. EMOTIONAL

SURVIVAL motivates the Protector, and LOVE AND BELONGING motivate the Nurturer. He needs to learn self-control because he frequently flies off the handle, though not necessarily in a violent way. Unfortunately being the caretaker that she is, the Nurturer won't stand up to him (at least not in the beginning). She will try to support him, and she will work to change him, but such changes rarely last.

She needs to let go of her attachment to others and find her own identity, two things the Protector cannot help her with. He may provide a sturdy home base from which she can work on her issues, but he won't understand what she is dealing with.

Wanting her attention focused on him, he may not like her helping other people so much. Anything physical is important to him, so when she physically takes care of others, he may get jealous.

She would be a great match for a protector, who pushes others away with his intense outbursts, because she won't leave him without giving him another chance. If he ever comes between her and those she cares about (or cares for), however, the sparks will fly.

THE PROTECTOR AND THE MATRIARCH

PHYSICAL VS. PHYSICAL

SURVIVAL motivates the Protector, and LOVE, BELONGING, AND RESPECT motivate the Matriarch. He needs to learn self-control because he frequently flies off the handle, though not necessarily in a violent way. She loves to be in control and won't be able to cope if he is so unpredictable.

She needs to commit to herself as much as she commits to her husband or family. With the Protector, she will spend a lot of time trying to make things perfect for him so he won't fly off the handle. She will take care of everything. In this way, he may take her for granted but he better not do it for long because he can only push her so far before she stands up for herself. Her marriage is important to her, and she won't give up easily, but 'home base,' in whatever form, is her domain.

He knows she does a lot for him, and he respects her for standing up to him. He takes it very seriously when she fights back because he knows he must have done something wrong to get her so angry.

She respects his space and knows he loves her, but she may do better with a more subservient man. On the other hand, a more powerful husband can set limits on her queendom, thus stopping her from taking over the kids' lives.

THE PROTECTOR AND THE MYSTIC

PHYSICAL VS. SPIRITUAL

SURVIVAL motivates the Protector, and an AESTHETIC NEED FOR BALANCE motivates the Mystic. He needs to learn self-control because he frequently flies off the handle, though not necessarily in a violent way. Teaching others how to control themselves is the Mystic's specialty. She won't respond to his intensity. She will always try to remain calm and unattached or sarcastic and flighty. Either way she won't accept his drama and that puzzles him.

She needs to learn to assert herself and to go out and experience life. As a strong man, the Protector can teach her to be assertive, but he will still want to look out for her and to protect her. Her nonviolent attitude allows him to do this.

He may be in awe of her spiritual and paranormal abilities, and he may even try to learn about them in detail. Maybe he can have the same experiences?

He's so physically focused that he may have a hard time believing in the unknown and things that are unseen. She respects a man who knows what he wants in life, however, the Protector is usually better at knowing what he doesn't want.

THE PROTECTOR AND THE FEMALE MESSIAH

PHYSICAL VS. SPIRITUAL

SURVIVAL motivates the Protector, and the AESTHETIC NEED TO BE CONNECTED TO SOMETHING GREATER motivates the Female Messiah. He needs to learn self-control because he frequently flies off the handle, though not necessarily in a violent way. She can help him with this, but he may not enjoy the way she goes about it. She can really push people to change.

She needs to learn to let go of the outcome of events and to trust what guides her. As long as he can stay in his role as protector he doesn't care where she is guided. As an asset he can help ensure her safety as she carries out her mission.

He can be a drawback if he refuses to take her seriously or believe in her. He can cause her to doubt herself and her task. He may also cause her to fear situations whether there is danger present or not.

She won't sit still for too long unless she's living in an oppressive society for women. This is just fine for the Protector. He loves to travel and move around. She just better not try to make him stop watching out for her, especially if he believes in her cause.

THE PROTECTOR AND THE MAIDEN

PHYSICAL VS. EMOTIONAL

SURVIVAL motivates the Protector, and SAFETY AND SECURITY motivate the Maiden. He needs to learn self-control because he frequently flies off the handle, though not necessarily in a violent way. She can help him relax and see the beauty in the world, but her naive nature will only bring out the Protector in him full force. She is his responsibility in his eyes, and he likes that.

She is very spontaneous and adventurous at times, and can share in his desire for travel and new experiences. He may not fly off the handle at all with her around because he feels she's too easygoing and innocent for that. He protects her from his outbursts.

She must learn to stand on her own two feet. The Protector wants to take care of her and isn't quick to teach her self-reliance. He is probably around much of the time so she doesn't have to be alone to figure out what's important to her.

The Protector may feel young again around her and enjoys showing off (especially his physical prowess) around her.

She looks up to him. He is the rock in her life and her personal defender. They clash if he lets his guard down and isn't there for her when she needs him.

THE RECLUSE AND THE SEDUCTIVE MUSE

SPIRITUAL VS. PHYSICAL

THE NEED TO KNOW AND UNDERSTAND motivates the Recluse, and SELF-ACTUALIZATION motivates the Seductive Muse. He needs to learn how to relate to people and to reconnect with his body. These are the Seductive Muse's specialties. She can teach him how to be more extroverted and how to enjoy the sensual side of life. She will enjoy teasing him.

She wants to be recognized for her brains, not just her looks. The Recluse is able to see a woman for her inner beauty instead of just her outer beauty. He will recognize her brains and her spirit within.

The Seductive Muse loves to be around people who are in touch with their body and their creative side. She loves to play and explore, and anything kinesthetic.

He may see her as a wonderful confidant. His whole world seems to open up when she is around. He never knew the physical world could hold so much beauty and wonder. He also likes her creative side because it comes from deep within, a place he's very familiar with. He will encourage the creative side within her.

She's not one to be the perfect stay-at-home wife. She may stay home but she's no June Cleaver.

The Recluse sees the Seductive Muse as fun and adventurous, but a little too intense for his taste at times. He knows she is not one to commit to, but he will enjoy her company all the same. The Seductive Muse loves a take-charge kind of guy, but the Recluse is not one to take charge. He will let her leave when she wants to. He may not know how to ask her to stay.

THE RECLUSE AND THE AMAZON

SPIRITUAL VS. PHYSICAL

THE NEED TO KNOW AND UNDERSTAND motivates the Recluse, and SURVIVAL motivates the Amazon. He needs to learn how to relate to people and to reconnect with his body. The Amazon can teach him how to rely on and develop his body, though not in the sensual ways the Seductive Muse teaches.

The Amazon wants to find a place of her own and to be recognized for her contributions. The Recluse completely understands this desire and may help her with it. He has always needed a home base that allows him privacy and solace.

If she ever gets intense, he won't respond to it. He will always try to remain calm and unattached or sarcastic and flighty. Either way he won't be sucked into her latest cause.

The Amazon is fine with a man who keeps to himself. She doesn't want to be obligated to go out for a night on the town or to make plans. She has more important things to do. Her causes keep her busy most of the time, though she is known for letting her hair down and enjoying herself.

The Recluse may not know how to act around the Amazon because he's so used to either being alone or dealing with needy people. She lets him be alone when he needs it and this is refreshing for him.

She likes her own space too and he's low maintenance in that vein. If she wants to go on a woman's camping trip for a week, he says no problem.

THE RECLUSE AND THE FATHER'S DAUGHTER

SPIRITUAL VS. MENTAL

THE NEED TO KNOW AND UNDERSTAND motivates the Recluse, and THE NEED TO KNOW AND UNDERSTAND motivates the Father's Daughter. He needs to learn how to relate to people and to reconnect with his body. These things are totally out of the Father's Daughter's league. The Recluse also needs to learn how to use his mind instead of his intuition/feelings all the time, however, and this is something the Father's Daughter can help him with. Reason and logic are her forte.

She needs to learn to let go of her inhibitions, to get back to nature, and to value herself as a woman. The Recluse can help her get her back into nature and maybe even help her value her womanhood, as he is not strongly gender identified. He sees a person's spirit, not his or her outward body. He can't help her overcome her inhibitions, however.

The Father's Daughter doesn't have much time to explore the unknown as the Recluse does. She may not have the patience for it and may not respect his choice to spend his time on it. She's used to office drama and business negotiations. She's also used to more assertive men. She can either admire or disrespect the Recluse for his easygoing attitude.

He has a hard time understanding all of the intellectual jargon she uses and wonders if she is trying to impress him or make him feel stupid. If he really likes her, he may start reading books on the subjects that interest her so they can talk about them. If she really likes him, she'll dabble in the unknown in an attempt to understand him better.

THE RECLUSE AND THE NURTURER

SPIRITUAL VS. EMOTIONAL

THE NEED TO KNOW AND UNDERSTAND motivates the Recluse, and LOVE AND BELONGING motivate the Nurturer. He needs to learn how to relate to people and to reconnect with his body. Being the Caretaker that she is, the Nurturer can help him with this. She will try to be understanding and give him the patience that he needs.

She needs to let go of her attachment to others and find her own identity. These are things the Recluse can help her with because he likes being alone himself. He won't like having their home filled with people all the time, however, and will keep her Nurturing in check by limiting visits from outsiders.

The Nurturer would be a great match for a Recluse who is afraid to be with others. She will always have people coming around, and the Recluse will never be lonely again. Deep down inside he may like this but won't admit it.

If he ever comes between her and those she cares about (or cares for), the tears will fall and he will feel guilty.

THE RECLUSE AND THE MATRIARCH

SPIRITUAL VS. PHYSICAL

THE NEED TO KNOW AND UNDERSTAND motivates the Recluse, and LOVE, BELONGING, AND RESPECT motivate the Matriarch. He needs to learn how to relate to people and to reconnect with his body. These are not things the Matriarch can teach, as she expects her man to bring home friends he's made at work. His friends are her friends.

She wants home base, and the Recluse probably is not the man to provide it for her. She loves to be in control and won't be able to cope if he is so easygoing and flighty, as she may see him.

She needs to commit to herself as much as she commits her husband or family. With the Recluse, she will probably have so little to do that she will be forced to spend time with herself.

Deep down inside he knows she does a lot for him and he respects her. He just has a hard time getting the alone time he needs. She seems to always want his attention, always nagging him and ordering him around, as if every free moment must be spent performing her chores. Her marriage is important to her and she won't give up easily but 'home base,' in whatever form, is her domain.

She tries to respect his space, usually unsuccessfully, and she knows he loves her but she may do better with a man who is more available than he is.

THE RECLUSE AND THE MYSTIC

SPIRITUAL VS. SPIRITUAL

THE NEED TO KNOW AND UNDERSTAND motivates the Recluse, and the AESTHETIC NEED FOR BALANCE motivates the Mystic. He needs to learn how to relate to people and to reconnect with his body. This is the same problem the Mystic has. She needs to learn to be assertive and to go out and experience life. They can either try to help each other learn these skills, or they can stay in their inner worlds.

These two are alike in temperament, but they may be different in belief systems or training, like a Monk and a Wiccan Priestess or a Hypnotherapist and a Psychic. This is where they can clash depending on how well they accept other belief systems. Have they had the same spiritual experiences?

They both may not want to take the time to get to know each other.

 ## THE RECLUSE AND THE FEMALE MESSIAH

SPIRITUAL VS. SPIRITUAL

THE NEED TO KNOW AND UNDERSTAND motivates the Recluse, and the AESTHETIC NEED TO BE CONNECTED TO SOMETHING GREATER motivates the Female Messiah. He needs to learn how to relate to people and to reconnect with his body. She can help him with this but he may not enjoy the way she goes about it. She can really push people to change.

She needs to learn to let go of the outcome of events and to trust what guides her. As long as he can have his alone time he doesn't care where she is guided. As an asset he can help her find safety as she carries out her mission. He may feel a sense of pride in her and her missions.

He can be a drawback if he refuses to take her seriously or believe in her. He can disappear and cause a lot of trouble for her.

She won't sit still for too long unless she's living in an oppressive society for women. On the other hand the Recluse needs a steady home base to build his sanctuary. He can be a very faithful husband and set up a home base for her to come back to when she needs it. He doesn't mind living alone for long periods of time at all and she may be gone often.

If he doesn't get sucked into her mission, he will likely leave her and the entire situation. He can easily walk away from others.

THE RECLUSE AND THE MAIDEN

PHYSICAL VS. EMOTIONAL

THE NEED TO KNOW AND UNDERSTAND motivates the Recluse, and SAFETY AND SECURITY motivate the Maiden. He needs to learn how to relate to people and to reconnect with his body. She can help him relax and see the beauty in the world. However, her naive nature may lose its appeal after a while and she may require too much attention.

She is very spontaneous and adventurous at times, but can also share in his desire for solitude. She can easily grasp all of his otherworldly interests and be a great conversationalist. But sooner or later she may get bored with his loner lifestyle.

She must learn to stand on her own two feet. The Recluse will push her to do that, as he doesn't want to be responsible for her. Even though he's around most of the time, he always doing his own thing.

She may look up to him, when he's around. If she has a crisis and he's not available, the sparks can fly when she sees him again. He won't be guilted; he can spot manipulation a mile away.

THE FOOL AND THE SEDUCTIVE MUSE

PHYSICAL VS. PHYSICAL

The NEED TO KNOW AND UNDERSTAND motivates the Fool, and SELF-ACTUALIZATION motivates the Seductive Muse. He needs to learn to set limits on his behavior and consider other people's feelings. She wants to be recognized for her brains, not just her looks. Neither of them can help the other with these tasks as the Seductive Muse loves to explore physically and the Fool will definitely see a woman for her looks before her brain.

The Fool likes being around someone who is uninhibited like the Seductive Muse but he doesn't like romantic entanglements. If he makes this clear up front, then she will accept it and they can have a good time.

She's not one to be the perfect stay-at-home wife. She may stay home but she's no June Cleaver. The Seductive Muse sees the Fool as easygoing, someone who will let her be as noncommittal as she wants to be. He may not have the take-charge personality that she craves.

She'll have her freedom with him if he is well adjusted and not the jealous type. If he gets jealous easily he will probably leave at the first sign of trouble. He's afraid to commit to someone—jealousy is the first sign that he's in too deep.

THE FOOL AND THE AMAZON

PHYSICAL VS. PHYSICAL

The NEED TO KNOW AND UNDERSTAND motivates the Fool, and SURVIVAL motivates the Amazon. He needs to learn to set limits on his behavior and consider other people's feelings. The Amazon can help him with that if she's willing to bother. She wants to find a place of her own and to be recognized for her contributions—the Fool doesn't care about finding a place of his own.

He may not know how to act around the Amazon. She may be tougher than he is, and this may make him feel like less of a man. Thus he may be short with her and uncooperative. He may see as too much of a challenge, or he may like the dominatrix type and seek her out. If she is very adventurous, they can get along well.

She has a hard time understanding his free spirit. She wonders how someone goes through life without making any plans at all. And why doesn't he care about my causes?

He may see her as too serious. He's not interested in fighting for a cause unless the task can be fun and adventurous—then he'll enthusiastically join in. She may mistake his help for deep concern for the cause and think they are very much alike. This sets her up for disappointment when he tells her his true reasons for joining the cause. He may not know how to care for the feelings of others. His behavior is not necessarily malicious.

THE FOOL AND THE FATHER'S DAUGHTER

PHYSICAL VS. MENTAL

The NEED TO KNOW AND UNDERSTAND motivates the Fool, and The NEED TO KNOW AND UNDERSTAND motivates the Father's Daughter. He needs to learn to set limits on his behavior and consider other people's feelings. These are things the Father's Daughter can teach him because she works with others all the time.

She needs to get back to nature, which is something the Fool can help her with. She also needs to value herself as a woman. The Fool can help her see the big picture regarding cultural stereotypes (he's antiestablishment), but he's not necessarily a feminist.

Though they are both motivated by the need to know and understand, the Father's Daughter approaches this need through books and the Fool through experience.

They are both very uncomfortable around each other. He knows nothing about the business world and doesn't want to learn. He is against all structure and rules, and hates the fact that one has to toil away at a job just for a place to sleep at night.

She doesn't understand his flighty, free-spirited nature. How can anyone live without knowing what the next day will bring? Her day planner is an all-important tool.

He is the biggest flirt that ever lived and she doesn't know how to flirt at all. He may find her charming at first if they meet where he can be in his element, for instance a bar or nightclub.

THE FOOL AND THE NURTURER

PHYSICAL VS. EMOTIONAL

The NEED TO KNOW AND UNDERSTAND motivates the Fool, and LOVE AND BELONGING motivate the Nurturer. He needs to learn to set limits on his behavior and consider other people's feelings. The Nurturer always considers what other people feel, so she can help him in this vein.

She needs to let go of her attachment to others and to find her own identity—something the Fool can help her with. He is so unpredictable that she will find herself on her own many times when she least expects it. There's not much for her to attach to and depend on with him. He's his own person.

The Fool may exploit her need to help others, simply by knowing she will always take him back into her life when he's down on his luck. She can't help herself. This is bad for her if she still has feelings for him.

He can't understand why she rearranges her entire life to help others. He admits that helping others is good but believes she needs to set boundaries for herself or she risks being of no use to anyone. He can teach her this.

She will be happy if his job has something to do with helping others, like working for the Peace Corps. This he may do as it allows him to move around a lot and meet new people. She may push his buttons if he's materialistic and unsympathetic with others. He better be able to deal with her giving attention to others.

THE FOOL AND THE MATRIARCH

PHYSICAL VS. PHYSICAL

The NEED TO KNOW AND UNDERSTAND motivates the Fool, and LOVE, BELONGING, AND RESPECT motivate the Matriarch. He needs to learn to set limits on his behavior and consider other people's feelings, and this will happen easily with the Matriarch in his life, if he stays around long enough. She loves to be in control and won't stand for him doing anything and everything he wants.

She needs to commit to herself as much as she commits to her husband or family. With the Fool she will probably overcompensate by watching his every move and keeping track of his every free minute. But she will also take care of everything at home, so he doesn't have to learn those responsibilities. This is what may drive him to stay with her.

He doesn't understand someone who is so driven to take part in the lives of others as she does. Such diligence takes too much time and effort, and in the meantime, your own life gets dull. Live and let live he says.

She doesn't respect him when he gets adventurous. She sees him as crazy for taking the risks that he takes. She will never join in with his risky undertakings unless an emotional incident pushes her over the edge. She shapes the lives of her family. They can't get on without her. Her worth comes from her family, and his worth comes from completing the tasks and risks he sets out to accomplish. He can be one of the biggest braggers.

THE FOOL AND THE MYSTIC

PHYSICAL VS. SPIRITUAL

The NEED TO KNOW AND UNDERSTAND motivates the Fool, and the AESTHETIC NEED FOR BALANCE motivates the Mystic. He needs to learn to set limits on his behavior and consider other people's feelings; these are the Mystic's specialties. She can teach him how to control himself and be more aware of others.

She needs to learn to be assertive and to go out and experience life. As a free spirit, he can teach her to enjoy life's pleasures, big and small. He can open up a whole new world for her and make it fun in the process. He can bring her out of her shell.

He may try to goad her into some crazy risks but if she complies she will be doing so for her own reasons and not to prove herself to him. She can't be manipulated like that.

He may be in awe of her spiritual and paranormal abilities, and he may even try to learn about them in detail. Maybe he can have the same experiences? What an adventure for him.

THE FOOL AND THE FEMALE MESSIAH

PHYSICAL VS. SPIRITUAL

The NEED TO KNOW AND UNDERSTAND motivates the Fool, and the AESTHETIC NEED TO BE CONNECTED TO SOMETHING GREATER motivates the Female Messiah. He needs to learn to set limits on his behavior and consider other people's feelings, and she can help him with this but he may not enjoy the way she goes about it. She can really push people to change.

She needs to learn to let go of the outcome of events and to trust what guides her. He is so used to letting go of outcomes that he can be a great teacher for her. He doesn't care if he believes in her mission or not, he can have a great time following her on her tasks. He can be an asset if he's willing to suspend his disbelief because he can help her take the risks she needs to take.

He can be a drawback if he refuses to take her seriously, or to believe in her, and shows it in his actions and words. He can cause her to hold on tighter to the outcome of her tasks if he pushes her too much. She may try to prove him wrong. He may not be serious enough for her taste though she enjoys being around happy people.

She won't sit still for too long unless she's living in an oppressive society for women. This fits well with the Fool, who finds work and structure boring. She always has a new agenda or cause to work for.

THE FOOL AND THE MAIDEN

PHYSICAL VS. EMOTIONAL

The NEED TO KNOW AND UNDERSTAND motivates the Fool, and SAFETY AND SECURITY motivates the Maiden. He needs to learn to set limits on his behavior and consider other people's feelings. These are things the Maiden needs to work on too so they may be too much alike for their own good. She is very spontaneous and adventurous at times, and captures his attention easily.

He may enjoy being the only risk taker because it makes him different, so he may not like her taking part in his adventures.

She must learn to stand on her own two feet. The Fool may not have the means to support her, and therefore she will have to become self-sufficient.

They won't necessarily be there for each other physically. He will be off playing around and so will she. But they can meet on an emotional level. They both share the same experiences and have a hard time fitting in with 'normal' society.

Both of them can feel validated and renewed in each other's company. They are kindred souls, however they may lack the resources to take care of themselves responsibly, unless one of them has come up with an invention or something of the sort that gives them a steady flow of income.

If she gets pregnant, things can get touchy for them. She will be forced to be responsible. He will also feel the pressure.

THE WOMAN'S MAN AND THE SEDUCTIVE MUSE

EMOTIONAL VS. PHYSICAL

LOVE AND BELONGING motivate the Woman's Man, and SELF-AC-TUALIZATION motivates the Seductive Muse. He needs to learn how to value himself as a man and to stop running away from responsibility. The Seductive Muse can help him value himself as a man, but she may not be able to teach him responsibility. She wants to be recognized for her brains, not just her looks, and the Woman's Man can definitely give that to her. He can always see a woman's inner beauty.

The Woman's Man likes to be around people who are playful and enjoy life. But he loves to find women who are inhibited or structured, and teach these things to them. He loves a 'project.' The Seductive Muse is not a good candidate for this because she is already playful and creative. They can be great friends and lovers for a long time. She won't need him the way the other archetypes may. She can stand on her own with men and is already in touch with her sexuality.

He feels like she understands him, like they operate on the same wavelength. He enjoys her creative bursts and may try to share in them. Just like her, he explores the physical senses and loves to dance. She's fun and outgoing.

She's not one to be the perfect stay-at-home wife. She may stay home but she's no June Cleaver. The Seductive Muse sees the Woman's Man as a great friend and/or lover. He is fun and adventurous and she knows he won't commit to her. This is fine. She sometimes has trouble committing to a relationship herself so she understands. She loves a take-charge kind of guy, and he's too emotional and easygoing for that.

THE WOMAN'S MAN AND THE AMAZON

EMOTIONAL VS. PHYSICAL

LOVE AND BELONGING motivate the Woman's Man, and SURVIVAL motivates the Amazon. He needs to learn how to value himself as a man and to stop running away from responsibility. The Amazon cannot teach him to value his manhood but she can teach him about self-respect. She can show him how to rely on and develop his body, but not in the sensual ways as the Seductive Muse would. He will most likely try to teach her how to be sensual.

The Amazon wants to find a place of her own and to be recognized for her contributions. The Woman's Man completely understands this, but he thinks finding one's inner child is much more important. He doesn't care about having a stable home base.

If she ever gets intense, he won't respond to it. He will always try to keep a playful attitude. Either way he won't be sucked into her latest cause. 'Life is too short,' he says.

She's fine with a man who keeps to himself, but he won't do that. He may want to change her, but she won't have it. She may think he uses women, the way he loves 'em and leaves 'em, but he does help the women he comes into contact with.

She likes her own space, and he can be high maintenance. If she wants to go on a woman's camping trip for a week, he may want to come along.

 ## THE WOMAN'S MAN AND THE FATHER'S DAUGHTER

EMOTION VS. MENTAL

LOVE AND BELONGING motivate the Woman's Man, and THE NEED TO KNOW AND UNDERSTAND motivates the Father's Daughter. He needs to learn how to value himself as a man and to stop running away from responsibility. These skills are right up the Father's Daughter's alley. She values men herself and she is used to being around responsible men.

She needs to learn to let go of her inhibitions, to get back to nature, and to value herself as a woman. The Woman's Man can help her with all these things. He lives a natural life, helps women loosen up and find themselves, and he values women. They can bring each other self-esteem and romance.

She is not very comfortable around him at first. He has a hard time understanding all of the intellectual jargon she uses, and he wonders if she is trying to impress him or make him feel stupid. She can be a good balance for him, but they will have a tough time making things work if she's too stubborn and unwilling to change. She's attracted to powerful men, and he isn't one. She may be too mentally focused for his taste, but he enjoys a 'project.'

She likes being the only woman in a man's life and he may have way too many female friends for her liking.

THE WOMAN'S MAN AND THE NURTURER

EMOTIONAL VS. EMOTIONAL

LOVE AND BELONGING motivate the Woman's Man, and LOVE AND BELONGING motivate the Nurturer. He needs to learn how to value himself as a man and to stop running away from responsibility. Being the Caretaker that she is, the Nurturer can help him value himself, but she may not be able to help him become more responsible. She will take care of things for him so he doesn't have many responsibilities.

She needs to let go of her attachment to others and to find her own identity—things the Woman's Man can help her with. He will drag her out, teach her how to have fun, and help her find what her own deep desires are. He will keep her caretaking side in check.

She understands his need to help women and will try to be understanding if he has a lot of female friends. He will understand her need to help others and will support her, unless this need takes over her life. He wants to see her enjoy her own life separate from being a caretaker.

He is very chivalrous and will bestow upon her some of the caretaking she bestows on others. This may make her uncomfortable at first, but it will do much to build her self-esteem.

THE WOMAN'S MAN AND THE MATRIARCH

EMOTIONAL VS. PHYSICAL

LOVE AND BELONGING motivate the Woman's Man, and LOVE, BE-LONGING, AND RESPECT motivate the Matriarch. He needs to learn how to value himself as a man and to stop running away from responsibility. She can teach him to be responsible, but she may do it in a way that makes him defensive; for example, she may give orders or ultimatums. She loves to be in control and won't be able to cope if he is so unpredictable.

She needs to commit to herself as much as she commits to her husband or family. She will probably spend much of her time attempting to make sure he doesn't walk out on her. She will take care of everything, and may feel like he's taking her for granted. If she does, look out because she will stand up for herself.

Marriage is very important to her, so if they are married, she won't give up easily on him. If they aren't married, she may be more lenient with him because she longs to be married.

Deep down inside he knows she does a lot for him and he respects her. He just wants her to let loose and enjoy life. He wants a playmate, not a matron.

She respects his playful nature and knows he loves her but she may do better with a more subservient man. On the other hand, a more powerful husband can set limits on her 'queendom,' thus stopping her from taking over the kids' lives.

She may secretly yearn to be more like the Woman's Man—carefree, playful, easygoing.

THE WOMAN'S MAN AND THE MYSTIC

EMOTIONAL VS. SPIRITUAL

LOVE AND BELONGING motivate the Woman's Man, and the AESTHETIC NEED FOR BALANCE motivates the Mystic. He needs to learn how to value himself as a man and to stop running away from responsibility. The Mystic is not the greater helper in this regard.

She needs to learn to be assertive and to go out and experience life. As an adventurous man, the Woman's Man can teach her to come out of her inner life and experience the senses.

He sees her as an easy woman to teach and mold. Since she's not invested in societal rules and expectations, she can easily accept his eccentric ways. She's just not used to playing around too much, even though she may be a very happy person. He can teach her to get in touch with her body and senses instead of numbing them in meditative pursuits. Gardening can be meditative, for instance.

He can be very supportive of her paranormal experiences. He may be in awe of her spiritual abilities, and he may even try to learn about them in detail. Maybe he can have the same experiences? He's always up for something new and exciting. They will do well if she reciprocates and shows interest in his hobbies.

THE WOMAN'S MAN AND THE FEMALE MESSIAH

EMOTIONAL VS. SPIRITUAL

LOVE AND BELONGING motivate the Woman's Man, and the AESTHETIC NEED TO BE CONNECTED TO SOMETHING GREATER motivates the Matriarch. He needs to learn how to value himself as a man and to stop running away from responsibility. She can help him do both, but he may not enjoy the way she goes about it. She can really push people to change.

She needs to learn to let go of the outcome of events and to trust what guides her. He is so against structure and planning that he can definitely help her with this. He may not be sure if he believes the same things she believes, but that doesn't matter to him. 'To each his own,' he says. If he's willing to suspend his disbelief, he can be an asset because he can help her go with the flow of events.

She sometimes becomes lost in her cause. He can teach her to get in touch with her physical senses and to see what the big deal is about being 'alive,' and to see why she shouldn't waste her lifetime ignoring her desires.

She won't sit still for too long unless she's living in an oppressive society for women. This is just fine for the Woman's Man. He loves moving around and meeting new people. He won't leave her as readily as other men might.

THE WOMAN'S MAN AND THE MAIDEN

EMOTIONAL VS. EMOTIONAL

LOVE AND BELONGING motivate the Woman's Man, and SAFETY AND SECURITY motivate the Maiden. He needs to learn how to value himself as a man and to stop running away from responsibility. This is not the Maiden's specialty. She needs to work on being responsible too, but that's because she acts 'young,' not because she's trying to live outside of society's rules.

She is also very spontaneous and adventurous at times and he may not see her as much of a project unless she has low self-esteem.

She must learn to stand on her own two feet. The Woman's Man can help her with this, encouraging her to be independent and pointing out all her good qualities. He's a real self-esteem booster.

They won't necessarily be there for each other physically. He will be off playing the field, and so will she. But they can meet on an emotional level. They both share the same experiences and have a hard time fitting in with 'normal' society.

They can both feel validated and renewed when together, but they also will likely be bored. He may not be able to teach her much, and she knows he isn't the marrying kind who will take care of her, which is what she really wants.

THE MALE MESSIAH AND THE SEDUCTIVE MUSE

SPIRITUAL VS. PHYSICAL

The AESTHETIC NEED TO BE CONNECTED TO SOMETHING GREATER THAN HIMSELF motivates the Male Messiah, and SELF-ACTUALIZATION motivates the Seductive Muse. He needs to learn to let go of the outcome of events, to trust what guides him, and to face his doubts. This is something the Seductive Muse can help with. She can teach him to go with the flow of life, and she can give him the confidence to face his doubts.

She wants to be recognized for her brains, not just her looks. The Male Messiah is able to see a woman for her inner beauty, to see beyond her exterior. He will recognize her brains and her spirit within, but will she recognize her own assets? He can help her with this, but she may not enjoy the way he goes about it. He can really push people to change.

The Seductive Muse loves to be around people who are in touch with their bodies and their creative sides. She loves to play and explore, and anything kinesthetic.

He may see her as a wonderful confidant. His whole world seems to open up when she is around. He never knew the physical world could hold so much beauty and wonder. She is a true muse to him.

Or he may see her as a deterrent—someone leading him astray when he wants to focus on his tasks.

She's not one to be the perfect stay-at-home wife. She may stay home but she's no June Cleaver. He isn't looking for a traditional family life. He may have one, but it doesn't top his list of desires.

She loves a take-charge kind of guy, which he is. But she wants someone who can be there for her, someone who will explore the sensual side of life with her. He's not so inclined.

The Male Messiah may see the Seductive Muse as fun and adventurous, but a little too intense for his taste. He doesn't know what to make of her at times and may feel a little off balance around her. If he has hangups about sex, they will clash.

 ## THE MALE MESSIAH AND THE AMAZON

SPIRITUAL VS. PHYSICAL

THE AESTHETIC NEED TO BE CONNECTED TO SOMETHING GREATER THAN HIMSELF motivates the Male Messiah, and SURVIVAL motivates the Amazon. He needs to learn to let go of the outcome of events, to trust what guides him, and to face his doubts. The Amazon can help him with these needs if she believes in what he is doing. She knows well how to trust that her work will get done; that is, that fighting for her causes will bring victory. She can't worry about outcomes when she knows things will work themselves out. She can trust others to do their jobs well, and she knows how to motivate them.

She wants to find a place of her own and to be recognized for her contributions. The Male Messiah may recognize her contributions, but he can't help her much in building a place of her own. He has other things on his mind.

They can both get behind a cause or task and work together for hours on end. They are like best friends most of the time. They understand how the other one thinks and feels. They understand commitment and perseverance.

She can help him by literally protecting him. She has the resources to do it.

If he needs to leave her, she will be okay with that. She can take care of herself and make it on her own. The Male Messiah needs a woman like that because he may leave or make sacrifices at any time.

THE MALE MESSIAH AND THE FATHER'S DAUGHTER

SPIRITUAL VS. MENTAL

THE AESTHETIC NEED TO BE CONNECTED TO SOMETHING GREATER THAN HIMSELF motivates the Male Messiah, and THE NEED TO KNOW AND UNDERSTAND motivates the Father's Daughter. He needs to learn to let go of the outcome of events, to trust what guides him, and to face his doubts. These things go against her ordered, planned lifestyle so she is not a good candidate for helping him achieve success.

She needs to learn to let go of her inhibitions, to get back to nature, and to value herself as a woman. He can help her get back to nature and to value herself, but she may not enjoy the way he goes about it. He can really push people to change. He can't teach her much about letting go of her inhibitions.

The Father's Daughter doesn't have much time to build causes and missions as the Male Messiah does. She may not have the patience for it and may not respect his choice to spend his time on it. She's used to office drama and business negotiations. She's used to smart, logical, and strong men. She can either admire or disrespect the Male Messiah for his choices. She certainly won't join him without a compelling reason.

He understands all of the intellectual jargon she uses but doesn't understand why she values the ability to use such big words all the time. What is the point?

If he really likes her, he may start reading about the subjects that interest her so they can talk about them. If she really likes him, she'll dabble in his tasks to try to understand him better. Still, they come from different worlds.

THE MALE MESSIAH AND THE NURTURER

SPIRITUAL VS. EMOTIONAL

The AESTHETIC NEED TO BE CONNECTED TO SOMETHING GREATER THAN HIMSELF motivates the Male Messiah, and LOVE AND BELONGING motivate the Nurturer. He needs to learn to let go of the outcome of events, to trust what guides him, and to face his doubts. The Nurturer is not skilled at letting go of her doubts. Because she is very committed to healing others, she's also not used to letting go of the outcome of events.

She needs to let go of her attachment to others and find her own identity. These are things the Male Messiah can help her with because he knows how to remain unattached.

He is also so unpredictable that she can't rely on him to be there for her all the time. There's not much for her to attach to and depend on with him, so she may look to others for this attachment rather than standing alone.

They both share the need to help others, which may keep them together for a long time. She understands where he is coming from but she simply can't let someone suffer for their higher good the way he can.

He understands why she rearranges her life to help others because he rearranges his life for his task or mission. They respect each other and can be great friends. He can be a very faithful husband.

THE MALE MESSIAH AND THE MATRIARCH

SPIRITUAL VS. PHYSICAL

THE AESTHETIC NEED TO BE CONNECTED TO SOMETHING GREATER THAN HIMSELF motivates the Male Messiah, and LOVE, BELONGING, AND RESPECT motivate the Matriarch. He needs to learn to let go of the outcome of events, to trust what guides him, and to face his doubts. These are not goals she can help him achieve because she may need to learn the same things.

She needs to commit to herself as much as she commits her husband or family. With the Male Messiah she will probably be too occupied trying to make sure he doesn't go off on a mission to examine what is truly important to her.

She loves to be in control and won't be able to cope if he is so unpredictable. She may try to hold him close by issuing ultimatums, but he won't be manipulated like that. He is perfectly fine on his own.

She will take care of everything and may feel like he's taking her for granted. Regardless, she may feel a sense of pride in how altruistic he is.

If they are married, she won't give up easily on him. Marriage is very important to her. If they aren't married, she may be more lenient with him because she longs to be married. Although he respects her feelings, he is not that interested in marriage. He may marry to have a solid home base, but marrying is not a goal of his.

She respects his drive to help others and knows he loves her but she may do better with a more subservient man. On the other hand a more powerful husband can set limits on her 'queendom,' thus stopping her from taking over the kids' lives.

THE MALE MESSIAH AND THE MYSTIC

SPIRITUAL VS. SPIRITUAL

THE AESTHETIC NEED TO BE CONNECTED TO SOMETHING GREATER THAN HIMSELF motivates the Male Messiah, and the AESTHETIC NEED FOR BALANCE motivates the Mystic. He needs to learn to let go of the outcome of events, to trust what guides him, and to face his doubts. These are things the Mystic can teach him. She lives in a receptive state, allowing everything that comes into her life to teach her something.

She needs to learn to be assertive and to go out and experience life. He's not one to experience much in life but he can teach her to be assertive. He's very driven when it comes to his missions.

These two are very easygoing people. They both want to join in something greater than themselves, but the Mystic needs more balance in her life and she will want time to herself. Going out into the world can be scary for her, and this is where they don't see eye to eye. She wouldn't mind that he goes away often, however, because she likes being alone.

She may see changing herself for the better as doing her part since she's setting the stage for others to heal themselves by example.

He needs to be more productive in his view, and he may not embrace her views.

THE MALE MESSIAH AND THE FEMALE MESSIAH

SPIRITUAL VS. SPIRITUAL

THE AESTHETIC NEED TO BE CONNECTED TO SOMETHING GREATER THAN HIMSELF motivates the Male Messiah, and the AESTHETIC NEED TO BE CONNECTED TO SOMETHING GREATER motivates the Female Messiah. He needs to learn to let go of the outcome of events, to trust what guides him, and to face his doubts.

She also needs to learn to let go of the outcome of events and to trust what guides her. Maybe together they can support each other and be there for the rough times. Sometimes seeing the bright side to someone else's problems helps you see the bright side to your own.

They can help each other carry out their missions. They may truly honor and respect each other. They have to be careful not to get too attached to each other, though. In this way, they can become a drawback for each other.

They can be great friends and offer much solace, as no one else may understand them or their actions. They are like soul mates, but they may never get to be together because their missions are always top priority.

Sometimes they have almost a psychic connection and can tell what the other one is doing across long distances.

THE MALE MESSIAH AND THE MAIDEN

SPIRITUAL VS. EMOTIONAL

THE AESTHETIC NEED TO BE CONNECTED TO SOMETHING GREATER THAN HIMSELF motivates the Male Messiah, and SAFETY AND SECURITY motivate the Maiden. He needs to learn to let go of the outcome of events, to trust what guides him, and to face his doubts. These are things the Maiden is great at. She is very spontaneous, adventurous, and trusting.

She must learn to stand on her own two feet. This will happen with the Male Messiah because she won't be top priority in his life. He will be off pursuing his tasks and most likely traveling distances away from her. This will push her to stand on her own two feet, as she will be alone most of the time and will have to figure out who she is and what her interests are.

Since he's not around much, he's fine with whatever she wants to do with her day. This is the kind of freedom she wants.

The Male Messiah can see her and her ways as a distraction. But she can also give him a lot of energy, strength, and confidence. She may be too innocent for him. He may not be able to talk to her about his day because he doesn't know if she can handle hearing about it. She is very sensitive and may be empathic.

THE ARTIST AND THE SEDUCTIVE MUSE

EMOTIONAL VS. PHYSICAL

SURVIVAL motivates the Artist, and SELF-ACTUALIZATION motivates the Seductive Muse. He needs to learn self-control and to distance himself from explosive situations. The Seductive Muse is very physical and probably should learn some self-control herself, so she's not a great candidate to teach him. She wants to be recognized for her brains, not just her looks, but being so visually oriented the Artist can't help but notice her looks.

The Artist loves to be around people who are in touch with their emotions, especially women. He loves to create works of art for himself and others. He is very intuitive, a visionary.

He may see the Seductive Muse as a wonderful playmate and confidant but he's afraid she may leave him. Maybe he feels he's not good enough for her. She understands him, and they can create beautiful works together. They operate on the same wavelength.

She's not one to be the perfect stay-at-home wife. She may stay home but she's no June Cleaver. The Seductive Muse sees the Artist as fun but a little too serious at times for her taste. She enjoys his company and loves a take-charge kind of guy, but his emotions may be too intense for her. He may get jealous.

THE ARTIST AND THE AMAZON

EMOTIONAL VS. PHYSICAL

SURVIVAL motivates the Artist, and SURVIVAL motivates the Amazon. He needs to learn self-control and distance himself from explosive situations. The Amazon can help him with that if they are doing physical tasks. She's also usually good at controlling her emotions.

She wants to find a place of her own and to be recognized for her contributions. The Artist may value what she does—he often gets his artistic/creative energy burst after being exposed to the harshness of life, so he can value her causes.

He may not know how to act around the Amazon. She may be tougher than he is. This may make him feel like less of a man, thus he may be short with her and uncooperative. He already may have a hard time fitting in with other men because he's so in touch with his emotions, and he doesn't want women to make him feel uncomfortable too.

She has a hard time understanding all the creative jargon he uses and wonders if he is trying to impress her or make her feel stupid. He can be a good balance for her, but they will have a tough time making things work if he's not assertive.

THE ARTIST AND THE FATHER'S DAUGHTER

EMOTIONAL VS. MENTAL

SURVIVAL motivates the Artist, and THE NEED TO KNOW AND UN-
DERSTAND motivates the Father's Daughter. He needs to learn self-control and to distance himself from explosive situations. This may be something she can help him with because she isn't an emotional person. She
can also teach him to use his mind instead of his emotional instinct all
the time.

She needs to learn to let go of her inhibitions, to get back to nature,
and to value herself as a woman. The Artist can't help her with these
things, but he can teach her to get in touch with her creative, intuitive
side which is more feminine.

They are not very comfortable around each other. He has a hard time
understanding all of the intellectual jargon she uses and wonders if she
is trying to impress him or make him feel stupid. She can be a good balance for him, but they will have a tough time making things work if she's
too assertive. She's attracted to powerful men, which he is, but he may
not be mentally focused enough for her taste.

She is not much of a muse for him, and he may get bored with her
corporate lifestyle and long hours at work. He can find many women who
would enjoy long hours with an artistic man.

THE ARTIST AND THE NURTURER

EMOTIONAL VS. EMOTIONAL

SURVIVAL motivates the Artist, and LOVE AND BELONGING motivate the Nurturer. He needs to learn self-control and to distance himself
from explosive situations. Being the Caretaker that she is, the Nurturer
won't create explosive situations, and she can help him deal with life and
his emotions.

She needs to let go of her attachment to others and find her own identity. The Artist may need a lot of attention so she will probably be attached

to him. If he works from home, they may be together a lot and she will have to deal with his emotional ups and downs.

She understands his creative side and will give him the space he needs when pursuing his interests. He will understand her need to help others and will support her, unless the need takes over her life. He may get jealous of the people she cares for.

He can be very intense and passionate and can teach her about caring deeply for another in a romantic way.

THE ARTIST AND THE MATRIARCH

EMOTIONAL VS. PHYSICAL

SURVIVAL motivates the Artist, and LOVE, BELONGING, AND RESPECT motivate the Matriarch. He needs to learn self-control and to distance himself from explosive situations. These are not things she can teach him, although she sure won't put up with outbursts for long.

She needs to commit to herself as much as she commits to her husband or family. The Artist may make her feel bad if she doesn't have interests of her own. He wants a creative type of woman who will understand his interests.

She wants a nice home base, and he's probably not the man to get it for her. He may not make enough money to support her and her dreams for a large family. Even if he does make enough money, he is probably too volatile a personality for her.

She loves to be in control and won't be able to cope if he is so emotional and erratic. She needs more stability. She also wants his friends to be her friends, but she'll have to take an interest in his creative pursuits if she wants to get to know his friends.

Deep down inside he knows she does a lot for him and he respects her. He just has a hard time dealing with her demands. "She's stifling my creativity," he thinks. To him she seems to always want his attention, always nagging him and ordering him around. Such annoyances can make it very difficult for him to work at home during the day if she's a homemaker.

Her marriage is important to her, and she won't give up easily, but 'home base,' in whatever form, is her domain. She tries to respect his space, usually unsuccessfully, and she knows he loves her, but she may do better with a man who is more available than he is.

THE ARTIST AND THE MYSTIC

EMOTIONAL VS. SPIRITUAL

SURVIVAL motivates the Artist, and the AESTHETIC NEED FOR BALANCE motivates the Mystic. He needs to learn self-control and to distance himself from explosive situations, both of which happen to be the Mystic's specialty. She can teach him self-control and to see the big picture when he gets upset.

She needs to learn to be assertive and to go out and experience life. As someone who sees a lot of beauty in the world, he can help bring her out of her shell. As someone who is willing to stand up to others, he can also teach her to be assertive.

Her quiet demeanor allows him to spend hours in her company. He may even want to make her the subject of his creative project.

She loves his creativity, for it comes from deep within the soul.

He may be in awe of her spiritual and paranormal abilities, and he may even try to learn about them in detail. Maybe the experience will help his creative work.

She enjoys her alone time so she's fine if he locks himself in his studio for hours or days at a time. He loves that about her, but sometimes he may try to get a rise out of her just for the sake of excitement.

THE ARTIST AND THE FEMALE MESSIAH

EMOTIONAL VS. SPIRITUAL

SURVIVAL motivates the Artist, and THE AESTHETIC NEED TO BE CONNECTED TO SOMETHING GREATER motivates the Female Messiah. He needs to learn self-control and to distance himself from explosive situations. She can help him with these things, but he may not enjoy the way she goes about it. She can really push people to change.

She needs to learn to let go of the outcome of events and to trust what guides her. The Artist is not skilled in these arenas. He doesn't care all that much about planning things out, but he's not a very trusting person either.

He can be an asset if he's willing to use his creative energy to help her. Otherwise, if he refuses to take her seriously or believe in her, he can be a drawback. He can cause her to doubt herself and her task.

She has a hard time understanding his projects and his 'selfishness,' as she sees it. She says things like: "What can one painting do for the world? Why is he always so moody? You're supposed to master your feelings, not be mastered by them."

She won't sit still for too long unless she's living in an oppressive society for women. That's okay for the Artist because as long as he can be himself and find time for his interests he likes a change of scenery once in a while. He wants a woman who will support and understand him, not try to change him.

THE ARTIST AND THE MAIDEN

EMOTIONAL VS. EMOTIONAL

SURVIVAL motivates the Artist, and SAFETY AND SECURITY motivate the Maiden. He needs to learn self-control and to distance himself from explosive situations. She can't help him with these things because she needs to learn the same lessons.

She needs to stand on her own two feet. The Artist wants to take care of her, but he can't always be emotionally available for her. He's focused on himself and his projects a lot. He is probably around much of the time so she doesn't have to be alone to figure out what's important to her.

She is very spontaneous and adventurous at times and can share in his desire for travel and new experiences. He may not bother with explosive situations with her around. She's too easygoing and innocent for that. She may captivate him.

The Artist can feel young again around her, and his creativity may sparkle again. She is another Muse. He may become too intense or passionate for her, starting arguments just to stir things up.

She enjoys his emotional side, and they can have many romantic nights together.

THE KING AND THE SEDUCTIVE MUSE

MENTAL VS. PHYSICAL

SELF-ESTEEM and SELF-RESPECT motivate the King, and SELF-AC-TUALIZATION motivates the Seductive Muse. He needs to feel vulnerable to change. The Seductive Muse can make him feel that way if he falls deeply in love with her, but sometimes a tragic event is what does it.

She wants to be recognized for her brains, not just her looks. Being so mentally focused, brains are what the King notices first.

The King loves to be around people who are strong and in control of their emotions. She can be very strong, but she is also very feeling and sensual. (The Femme Fatale can really cause him trouble!)

He may see her as a wonderful playmate and confidant. He feels like she understands him, like they operate on the same wavelength, until she goes into creative mode. He doesn't pursue his creative side. It's too emotional. He's too much in control for that. She's fun and outgoing.

She's not one to be the perfect stay-at-home wife. She may stay home but she's no June Cleaver. The Seductive Muse sees the King as a great provider but a little too serious for her taste. She knows he's not the most faithful man, but she will enjoy his company all the same. She loves a take-charge kind of guy, and he can definitely take charge—of everything.

THE KING AND THE AMAZON

MENTAL VS. PHYSICAL

SELF-ESTEEM and SELF-RESPECT motivate the King, and SURVIVAL motivates the Amazon. He needs to feel vulnerable to change, and sometimes a tragic event is what does it. The Amazon can make him feel vulnerable, if she's strong around him and acts like his equal.

She wants to find a place of her own and to be recognized for her contributions. The King will value what she does, but he's looking for the perfect woman to settle down with. He's better off with someone more subservient so there will be less fighting at home. He wants his home to be his sanctuary.

She doesn't want to be protected or saved. She wants to do that herself. He's willing to let her save herself, but he will always see her as a somewhat silly woman for being so assertive. If she messes up even in the slightest, he will laugh with her and at her.

He may not know how to act around the Amazon because he's so used to having people grovel around him, and she won't do that.

She gets frustrated if he condescends to her. He will never see her as an equal, but thinks it's cute how she tries so hard. Such opinions really push her buttons.

THE KING AND THE FATHER'S DAUGHTER

MENTAL VS. MENTAL

SELF-ESTEEM and SELF-RESPECT motivate the King, and THE NEED TO KNOW AND UNDERSTAND motivates the Father's Daughter. He needs to feel vulnerable to change, and sometimes a tragic event is what does it. The Father's Daughter will never make him feel vulnerable, but she is used to being around powerful men.

She needs to learn to let go of her inhibitions, to get back to nature, and to value herself as a woman. The King can't help her with any of this. He likes women who are in control and mentally focused. The Father's Daughter is like this.

They are very comfortable around each other and can be business partners. He can work with women who show they know what they are doing. The Father's Daughter has much experience working with men.

She's attracted to powerful men, which the King is, plus he is as mentally focused as she is. The problem for this pairing comes when he wants to settle down and build a home and family—his kingdom. She wants to continue working. Her career is number one in her life, not kids. She usually won't give into his demands and if she does it may hurt her in the long run.

She likes being the only female in the group, and feels she is the 'exceptional woman.' "The King may not be able to work with other women but I'm different," she tells herself. She expects him to give her respect and to see her as an asset.

 THE KING AND THE NURTURER

MENTAL VS. EMOTIONAL

SELF-ESTEEM and SELF-RESPECT motivate the King, and LOVE AND BELONGING motivate the Nurturer. He needs to feel vulnerable to change, and sometimes a tragic event is what does it. The Nurturer can't make him feel vulnerable. Being the Caretaker that she is, the Nurturer won't stand up to the King. She will always try to be understanding with him because she sees the kind of day he's had.

She needs to let go of her attachment to others and to find her own identity—not things the King can help her with since he often encourages people to depend on him. His attitude is, "I'll provide everything."

He may not like her helping other people so much. He feels her attention should be focused on him, and that these people are taking advantage of her. He may say, "She should be paid. She should be rewarded. She should take care of herself more." He'll never understand her, and he may do better with a woman who is stronger than the Nurturer but more subservient to him.

She would be a great match for a King who pushes others away with his demands and rulership. She doesn't want to leave him without giving him another chance. They can be a great match.

Very few people take the time to understand and stick by him. Most of them do it out of fear, she can do it out of love. He never may have known real love before, and her nurturing can touch his heart.

 THE KING AND THE MATRIARCH

EMOTIONAL VS. PHYSICAL

SELF-ESTEEM and SELF-RESPECT motivate the King, and LOVE, BELONGING, and RESPECT motivate the Matriarch. He needs to feel vulnerable to change, and sometimes a tragic event is what does it. The Matriarch can't make him feel vulnerable.

She needs to commit to herself as much as she commits to her husband or family. With the King, she will be kept busy running their home as well as he runs their 'business.' She will take care of everything. In this way he may take her for granted, and he better change his ways because she will stand up for herself. He can only push her so far. Her marriage is important to her, and she won't give up easily, but 'home base,' in whatever form, is her domain. He need be careful not to devalue her contribution to their partnership.

Deep down inside he knows she does a lot for him and he respects her for standing up to him. He takes her very seriously when she does, as he knows he must have done something wrong to get her so angry.

She respects the King's space and knows he loves her, but she may do better with a more subservient man. On the other hand, a more powerful husband can set limits on her 'queendom,' thus stopping her from taking over the kids' lives.

They are both so much alike that they clash often, but they also understand each other and may be the only other person to put up with the other. They can be best friends and truly respect each other—when they aren't driving each other crazy.

THE KING AND THE MYSTIC

MENTAL VS. SPIRITUAL

SELF-ESTEEM and SELF-RESPECT motivate the King, and AESTHETIC NEED FOR BALANCE motivates the Mystic. He needs to feel vulnerable to change, and sometimes a tragic event is what does it. The Mystic is not one to make him feel vulnerable unless he falls in love with her.

She needs to learn to be assertive and to go out and experience life. As a very strong and powerful man, the King can teach her to be assertive, but it's more likely that he will be assertive for her and she will feel cared for.

If he is going through a midlife crisis of some sort, or just looking for a change, she will be a wonderful mystery to him. She can change his whole world, maybe even bring him in touch with his spirituality.

He may be in awe of her spiritual and paranormal abilities. They may offer a great escape from his day-to-day grind, and he will look forward to seeing her. She's so different from everyone else he deals with every day.

He probably won't believe in anything but science. For him, it must be proven to be real. This is where they can clash, especially if he attacks her core beliefs. She can't understand why he does what he does for a living. She would never want so much responsibility, and she's not one to play house for someone so demanding.

THE KING AND THE FEMALE MESSIAH

MENTAL VS. SPIRITUAL

SELF-ESTEEM and SELF-RESPECT motivate the King, and an AESTHETIC NEED TO BE CONNECTED TO SOMETHING GREATER motivates the Female Messiah. He needs to feel vulnerable to change and sometimes a tragic event is what does it. She can help him change, but he may not enjoy the way she goes about it. She can really push people.

She needs to learn to let go of the outcome of events and to trust what guides her. He is so used to structure and planning that he can't help her with this at all. He's not even sure he believes what she believes in. At first it may seem funny to him, but sooner or later he'll expect her to calm down and find a new direction in life.

If he's willing to suspend his disbelief, he can be an asset because he can help her make a plan and get people together to carry out that plan.

He can be a drawback if he refuses to take her seriously or believe in her. He can cause her to doubt herself and her task. He may also try to do everything for and take control of the situation. He won't do things her way, though, and that's the problem.

She won't sit still for too long unless she's living in an oppressive society for women. This doesn't fit well with the King, who wants to build a mini kingdom at home.

She always has a new agenda or cause to work for, and the King can't deal with that. Either he is the number one thing in her life or it's over.

THE KING AND THE MAIDEN

MENTAL VS. EMOTIONAL

SELF-ESTEEM and SELF-RESPECT motivate the King, and SAFETY AND SECURITY motivate the Maiden. He needs to feel vulnerable to change and sometimes a tragic event is what does it. She can help him relax and see the beauty in the world, but her naive nature will only bring out the King in him full force. She is his responsibility and under his control.

She is very spontaneous and adventurous at times, and can show him a great time if they travel. He may not be too demanding with her at first, she's so easygoing and innocent, and she won't challenge him outright. He tries to protect her from the harshness of life.

She needs to stand on her own two feet. The King wants to take care of her and isn't quick to teach her self-reliance. He can feel young again around her and enjoys showing her off. She is his possession, and he doesn't think she can live without him. She's more resourceful than he thinks.

She looks up to him. He is the rock in her life and her personal defender. They clash if he lets his guard down and isn't there for her when she needs him.

After a while, his demands may change her. She may become harsh or jaded, and if so, he will wonder where the sweet woman went. Eventually she will learn to stand up to him.

ROMANTIC TENSION

At this point you have a great understanding of all the archetypes and how they interact with each other. Why are romantic interactions important? Because love is universal.

Romance novels make up the largest market in the industry for a reason! Most of the highest paid authors are romance novelists. In fact millions of women devour romance novels in an effort to receive the love and romance they can't find in their everyday relationships. Truth is we all are interested in love, which is why even manly action films have a love interest in them as a rule. There are very few films made without some sort of love interest.

Now that we've discussed the interactions between the sexes, I'd like to mention the three types of intimate scenes that exist. They are called Anticipation, Submission, and Empowerment.

Anticipation occurs when the lovers want to be together but can't, so they anticipate being with each other. Usually there's an obstacle keeping them apart, and this obstacle creates anticipation in the reader as well. "When will they get to be together?"

ARCHETYPES THAT FALL INTO THE ANTICIPATION SCENE EASILY:

FEMALE: Amazon, Father's Daughter, Maiden, Mystic, Female Messiah

MALE: Businessman, Recluse, Fool, Male Messiah

For these archetypes, a job or other main focus will keep the attention on things other than the relationship, thus causing problems for the couple. This "distraction" may also keep the pair apart much of the time. For some of these archetypes, someone else has authority over his or her life, for example the Maiden and Fool, preventing them from running off to see their beloveds. In such situations, great longing can set in as well as deep fantasizing.

Submission means one person loves the other so much she or he would do anything to see that love returned. They will submit to almost any demand or requirement. Examples include the mistress who waits for years for her lover to leave his wife and the hero who has to prove himself to win over the heroine. The question is, "Will he find his love returned?"

ARCHETYPES THAT FALL INTO THE SUBMISSION SCENE EASILY:

FEMALE: Seductive Muse, Nurturer, Matriarch, Maiden

MALE: Protector, Woman's Man, Artist

These archetypes are usually more focused on their 'objects of affection' rather than on their careers or daily living. They can be very emotionally vulnerable and easily taken advantage of.

Empowerment occurs when gender positions become reversed. In many cases, this means the woman gains a powerful position. She calls the shots, not because her male counterpart is submissive, but because she is willing to walk away from him if she has to. In most situations men have more power over circumstances than women do. It's not unusual for a man to leave a woman so that he can do his job—just watch a typical western—but it is unusual for a woman to walk away for the same reason. The question becomes, "Will she leave him?" On the flip side the man can also decide to walk away from a woman, when he finds his own empowerment. A good example is the dentist character in *The Hangover*.

ARCHETYPES THAT FALL INTO THE EMPOWERMENT SCENE EASILY:

> **FEMALE:** Seductive Muse, Amazon, Father's Daughter, Mystic, Female Messiah, Maiden

> **MALE:** Any male archetype

These archetypes can be very independent. They know how to build an identity of their own. They can separate from their lover and still be secure with themselves. The Seductive Muse may need another mate waiting in the wings before she can walk away, but she can still be strong enough to do it.

You will use this information later when you start plotting your character's romantic story arc or subplot. For now I want you to write a love letter between your two main characters. You may be pleasantly surprised at what you discover about your character's psyche and past history as you do this exercise.

EXERCISE:

Write love letters between your hero and heroine when they first meet. Who would write the first letter? Who is the pursuer? Who is able to express their feelings? How does the heroine perceive what the hero has written, and vice versa?

Now write love letters that take place after the couple has shared an intimate moment. Then write one that takes place after the story is over.

If you prefer, you can write a love letter from one of your characters to another character who isn't in your story. The hero can be in love with a woman who has passed away, for example, and the letter can be to her.

Paint a very vivid picture of how your characters feel, even if they would never give this letter to their loved one.

Show their sense of loneliness, loss, anticipation, or awe. If you speak from your heart and not your head you can write such letters yourself and use them to inspire your novel writing.

If you are an action writer and this is hard for you, think of *Lethal Weapon* and how Mel Gibson told the story of his wife's death to his partner.

- Try not to be obvious with your words.

- Paint a picture of how the character feels using metaphors. Think about using all the senses: sight, smell, taste, hearing, and feeling.

- Take a walk in a natural setting or listen to music to get in the mood and into the character's feelings.

- What would your character say if no one was going to read the letter?

Now read the letters and see what this tells you about your characters. If your character is reluctant to talk, consider why this is so. If your character blabs on and on about herself, consider why this is so.

Did you find another layer of subtext to add to their backstories? Use these letters later on to develop your love scenes.

WRITING ABOUT LOVE

Love is a hard subject for most people to handle. It brings up our insecurities, makes us feel vulnerable, and subjects us to the possibility of deep pain.

All great works of fiction have some sort of romantic theme within them. Love is universal. Love is something everyone desires to have in their life.

ACTION STORY WRITERS

Some of you may be writing action stories and are wondering why you need to read this part of the book. Again. Love makes the world go around. How many heroes get the girl in the end? Many! Sometimes their motivation is to get the girl, or at least impress her. He doesn't do this for just mere sex and often finds meaningless sexual relationships along his journey.

In these more manly stories, the romantic plot may take a backseat to the main storyline, but the stages listed in the following pages show up in the story on some level, even if it only takes place on one page in your script or novel.

ROMANCE WRITERS

Some of you may be writing romance novels and wondering how the masculine and feminine journeys I presented in 45 *Master Characters* (or the Joseph Campbell model) fit with the romantic journeys. Well, if you want to write a great romance, you should start with a traditional journey model as the plan for your main plot and use the romantic journeys as a plan for the subplot. This doesn't mean the romance will take a backseat to the main story. Romances are supposed to be about romance after all.

The main story becomes the spine on which the relationship is developed. Remember the traditional journeys are very suitable to character-driven stories where the hero will face many obstacles to her goal and have to face hardships. The elements of the romantic journeys become the hardships. You can create an adventure plot and weave the romantic subplot into it.

Think of it this way: Most of Barbara Cartland's romance novels (which have collectively sold over a billion copies) are similar to the Cinderella romance model—the pretty, quiet, innocent girl meets the handsome, powerful, older man who is usually a cynic. He falls in love with her and molds her into a beautiful princess, teaching her the art of love by the end of the story.

At the same time, though, most of Cartland's novels take place in exotic places and feature heroes who explore exotic lands, intent on saving the world. She purposely 'added a touch of James Bond' as she put it, to all her stories.

WHO SAID ROMANCE HAS TO BE BORING?

By analyzing the top three fairy tales—*Cinderella*, *Beauty and the Beast*, and *Sleeping Beauty*—you will see firsthand how to plot the romantic journey or subtext of your story. Fairy tales are universal, just as archetypes are. These stories are found in different variations across many cultures.

Very often in real life, love and power are intertwined. When you love someone, you are left vulnerable to the object of your desire. Likewise, when someone else loves you, you are placed in the more powerful position.

In the three fairy tales that follow you will find three variations of how love and power manifest themselves in relationships. The suggested archetypes are not meant to be the rule, they are simply the archetypes that fit most easily into each romantic subplot. Mixing archetypes a bit may make it more interesting.

CINDERELLA

In the *Cinderella* romantic journey, the heroine falls in love with the hero first and she is left at his mercy, even if she is an Amazon at heart. Her actions are centered around him and whether or not he will save her. Very often these stories focus on the hero and how he's feeling. Hamlet and Ophelia come to mind.

ROMANTIC THEMES:

> **RAGS TO RICHES:** Getting your due against all obstacles. To go from a place of lack and dissatisfaction to a place of abundance and happiness. She's earned it.

> **ROMANTIC RESCUE:** Saving your partner from self-destruction, or needing to be saved or nursed back to health yourself. Love is life-saving and life changing on a physical, emotional, mental, or spiritual level.

CINDERELLA ARCHETYPES: Nurturer, Maiden

PRINCE ARCHETYPES: Protector, Woman's Man, King

Some variations on this story are *Cinder-Helle* by Barbara Walker and *Tale of the Shoe* by Emma Donoghue.

BEAUTY AND THE BEAST

In the *Beauty and the Beast* romantic journey, the hero falls in love with the heroine first and is left at her mercy. The story often focuses on how the heroine is feeling. The hero is usually an extremely powerful man in every area of his life except where the heroine is concerned. Very often his whole life depends on her decision to love him back and save him from his meek existence. *The Phantom of the Opera* comes to mind.

Romantic Themes:

INDEPENDENCE: Desire for someone different than the people you have previously dated or desire for someone completely different from you. Wanting a life change and needing someone who is where you may want to go.

LOVE VS. HONOR: What you want to do versus what you should do. Considering others' needs and your duty to your family. There is a major obstacle in your relationship and you have to learn to value your own needs. This fits well with paranormal stories as the hero is usually otherworldly and 'normal' people and family members may not accept him.

BEAUTY ARCHETYPES: Seductive Muse, Amazon, Matriarch

BEAST ARCHETYPES: Recluse, King, Protector, Artist

Variations on this story include *Ugly and the Beast* by Barbara Walker and *Tale of the Rose* by Emma Donoghue.

SLEEPING BEAUTY

In the *Sleeping Beauty* romantic subplot, both the heroine and hero fall in love at the same time, a situation that puts them on equal footing. They save each other through their mutual love. Romeo and Juliet comes to mind.

Romantic Themes:

LOVE CONQUERS ALL: You need someone to help you gain the courage to face yourself and your inner demons so you can heal. (Example: The hero has a drug addiction.) There's a tug between desire for the love of your life and a fear of commitment. Other things try to take precedence over the relationship.

SECOND CHANCES: You try to recapture lost love and want to go back to a specific time in your life when things were better. This new person is a chance to recapture what you are missing in your life.

SLEEPING BEAUTY ARCHETYPES: Father's Daughter, Mystic, Female Messiah, Amazon

PRINCE ARCHETYPES: Businessman, Male Messiah, Fool, Woman's Man

Variations on this story include *The Tale of the Needle* by Emma Donoghue.

VARIATIONS ON A THEME

Of course variations on a theme always exist. The following outlines of the above fairy tales are not hard and fast rules, just interesting guidelines that can help inspire you. They can be used as a sort of road map as you plot your story.

CINDERELLA: THE HERO HOLDS THE POWER.

"Rags to Riches" and "Romantic Rescue"

Unlike the two story models that follow this one, *Cinderella* gives full power to the hero as he rescues the heroine and changes her life.

- The Prince is going to throw a ball; it's time for him to find a wife.

- Cinderella is in a bad state of affairs. Her parents have died and she has no one to look after her except her nasty stepmother.

- Everyone but Cinderella is going to the ball. She has nothing to wear.

- A fairy helps her go to the ball, allowing Cinderella's outer beauty as well as inner beauty to shine forth.

- She goes to the ball and meets the Prince but has to leave at midnight or her whole world will fall apart. The Prince falls in love with her the moment he sees her.

- The Prince decides that Cinderella is the one for him and he stops at nothing to find her.

- The Prince finally finds her, proposes marriage, and changes her life. He will care for her now. He has saved her from her mean stepmother and sisters. He will teach her what a real family is all about.

Cinderella is an innocent heroine who has all the qualities the hero thought he'd never find in one woman. She is set apart from all the other women in the land. She is a special girl who needs to be schooled in the arts of love, and the hero is the only man who is up to the job.

She goes out and meets the hero but doesn't expect much to happen. She runs away from him, and he enjoys the chase, determined to have her whether she wants him or not. She is often much younger than her pursuer and more inexperienced. She grows and blossoms because of his influence and help. He saves her. Often these stories are written from the hero's perspective.

This story focuses on the hero falling in love with the heroine, since she's in love with him from the start.

The Cinderella Journey:

ACT I

- We meet the hero and learn about his unhappiness or cynical look at life.

- We meet the heroine and see how desperate her life situation is. We also learn how exceptional she is compared to other women.

- They meet each other, and she falls in love with him.

ACT II

- A task or situation forces them to be together.

- He is skeptical and unsure of their relationship. He may try to send her away.

- He realizes he loves her, too, but obstacles and insecurity keep them apart.

ACT III

- He finally goes out and gets her. He saves her with his love.

- He teaches her about love and family and life.

- They live happily ever after.

BEAUTY AND THE BEAST: THE HEROINE HOLDS THE POWER.

"Independence" and "Love vs. Honor"

In *Beauty and the Beast*, the heroine saves the hero.

- Beauty asks her father for a rose when he goes out of town.

- Her father gets stuck in a storm and finds shelter in a strange castle.

- When he leaves, he picks a rose and the Beast comes out to yell at him and demands his life in payment.

- The Beast agrees to take Beauty as payment instead.

- Beauty agrees to live with the Beast to save her father.

- Beauty and the Beast become friends, but Beauty can't agree to marry him.

- Beast allows Beauty to go home to visit her sick father if she agrees to return in seven days.

- She forgets to return and the Beast gets sick without her. Beauty rushes back to his side to pronounce her love for him.

- The Beast is saved by her love and turned into a handsome prince.

The focus on this story is on the heroine and how she feels. She has to fall in love with the hero of her own free will. He cannot force himself upon her. He doesn't live in the normal world and can't make any claims upon her. Society's rules do not apply to him.

The Beast demands her in payment regardless of how she looks or who she is, sight unseen. He is not looking for the best woman in all the land but any woman who can truly love him for who he is.

Power, tension, and violence set the tone in this **gothic-style story**. The Beast is like a child and Beauty holds the power to save him. She is the light to his darkness. She changes his life for the better in the end and he feels unworthy of her.

This story focuses on the heroine falling in love with the hero, since he is already in love with her from the start.

The Beauty and the Beast Journey:

ACT I

- We meet the heroine and see how stable her life is, good or bad.

- An obstacle or chance meeting brings her in contact with the hero. He seems rough around the edges and is often a loner.

- The hero immediately falls in love with her for who she is, not because of her looks.

ACT II

- A task or situation forces them to be together.

- She is hesitant about their relationship.

- He does something so wonderful, thoughtful, or protective that she starts to fall in love with him.

- Obstacles keep them apart.

ACT III

- The hero is in trouble and she saves him with her love.

- They live happily ever after.

SLEEPING BEAUTY:
BOTH THE HERO AND HEROINE HOLD THE POWER.

"Love Conquers All" and "Second Chances"
Of the three stories outlined here, *Sleeping Beauty* walks the middle road, where the hero and heroine are true equals sharing in the same type of fate before they meet each other.

- Sleeping Beauty is the victim of a curse.

- No one can help her but the good fairy who changes the wicked spell of death put upon her. Beauty sleeps instead of dies and all the royal servants are put to sleep with her.

- The Prince, wandering the lands in search of something he can't name or find, happens upon her castle and enters.

- He finds her sleeping and falls in love with her. His whole world changes as he realizes this feeling of true love is what he was seeking all along.

- He kisses her and she awakens. She had been dreaming of him and waiting for him for centuries and is so happy he is here. They get married.

Both the hero and heroine are in dire straights. They are both 'asleep' before their chance meeting, lost in waiting and longing for something more. The Prince did not know what ailed him until he laid eyes upon her and felt love course through his heart.

They fall in love at the same time, and they both grow from the union. They are very much alike and on equal footing. Very often these stories use plot to keep the couple separated and battling obstacles.

This story focuses on the couple being able to stay together, since they fall in love with each other right away.

The Sleeping Beauty Journey:

ACT I

- The innocent heroine is a victim of fate. There's a stain on her perfect world.

- She feels lost and alone with no hope for anything better. Or she doesn't even know there is a problem until she meets the Prince later on and feels what true happiness is.

- Others come along and try to help her but it doesn't work.

- The wandering hero, who feels like something is missing goes about his life.

ACT II

- Something catches his eye and decides to go after it, taking a big risk.

- He finds the heroine and they both feel true happiness.

- Both of their lives are completely changed by this love. They are two completely different people than they were in the beginning of the story.

ACT III

- They fall deeper in love and make their plans, regardless of what others think.

- They are determined to be together regardless of the cost.

WRITING LOVE SCENES

Just as your main story has a beginning, middle, and end so should your intimate love scenes. Outline the intimate relationship between your characters. Does it follow the normal progression of falling in love? Is there a beginning, middle, and end?

Do they go from falling in love at first sight to a series of chaste dates and then marriage? Do they hate each other at first? Is the heroine aggressive?

As a romance author, you have several decisions to make up front regarding sex and love.

SEX AND LOVE

When it comes to sex, you must decide how intimate your hero and heroine will be with each other and how often they will be together. If they won't be together until the end, you have to plan enough obstacles to keep them apart throughout the story.

With love, you have to decide if your hero will be in touch with his feelings or not. If he will be able to express his feelings to the heroine, at what point in the story does this happen?

When writing romance you need to decide what your philosophy is. What are the moral standards you live by? Or do you want to write sex scenes that border on erotica? Think about it and make a decision so you can feel more comfortable as you write.

- What belongs in the forbidden zone to you?
- What would you never do with a man or woman you just met? Or a man or woman you've known for thirty years?
- Do you think sex can ever be Divine?
- Can your characters make love with words instead of deeds?
- Do your characters have to be married before they can be intimate? What time period are you writing in?
- Will the heroine be aggressive like the Seductive Muse may be? Or uncomfortable like the Matriarch may be?
- Will the hero prefer physical contact right away like the Protector might? Or will he like to look at the heroine for hours like the Artist might?

When you are developing your idea and outlining your story, think about how many sex scenes your book will have. Instead of jumping into a sex scene right away, start off with more sensual scenes and gradually get 'steamier' as the story moves along.

Once you're naked, you're naked. Savor the moments between your lovers. Stop and take a good look at your intimate scenes.

- Have you thought about the desires of your hero and heroine?
- What details are you missing?
- What small gestures can be a source of sensuality? Think of the details. Which is better? "A man puts his arm around a woman?" OR "A masculine hand caresses the small curve of a woman's back?"

Consider writing your loves scenes using all the senses. When writing a love scene, you must not only think about setting and character arcs, you must remember to use all the senses especially as they apply to the setting.

It's very simple, really, just take a look at the location of your love scene and examine it from the perspective of the senses.

- Seeing
- Smelling
- Tasting
- Hearing
- Feeling

Seeing:

- How does the heroine look? The hero?
- How does the hero look to the heroine?
- Where are they?
- What does the setting look like?
- Does the heroine see something that distracts her from the hero? Does this bring up a good or bad memory for her?
- How is the lighting?

Describe love as if it were a color. Use a metaphor: "As blue as the ocean."

Smelling:

- Does the hero smell of musk and cologne?
- Are there flowers nearby? Did he buy them for her?
- Is someone cooking nearby?
- Are they near the ocean, and she can smell the ocean breeze?

Describe love as if it were a smell. "The sweet scent of a rose in the morning dew."

Tasting:

- Are they eating together? Does he feed her from his own plate?
- How do his kisses taste to the heroine?
- Does she 'sour' as he walks away? Or 'sweeten' as he comes near?
- Does everything taste better when she is around?

Describe love as if it were a taste. "Her lips tasted of honey and wine."

Hearing:

- Do they talk during lovemaking?
- Does she cry out?
- Is there music playing in the background?
- What noises are in the setting?
- Does the cry of a wolf scare her and send her into the hero's arms?
- Can they hear others approaching nearby?

Describe love as if it were a sound. "…the flutter of birds overhead, soaring into the night sky."

Feeling:

- How does the heroine feel? The hero?
- How does it feel to the heroine to be naked?
- How does his body feel to her? His hand?
- What type of fabrics are in the room?
- Is the furniture soft or lumpy?
- Can she feel or sense his desire?

- Does the light make it feel warm and inviting? Or mysterious?
- How's the temperature?

Describe love as if it were a feeling. "The butterflies in her stomach quickly turned into bees as he drew her near."

ANIMAL ARCHETYPES

ANIMALS AS ARCHETYPES

"Nothing can be truly beautiful if it has no function, so what's the point in making art that has no message, telling stories that have no value, that serve no function for us." —Russell Brand

Whether you are writing a character-driven piece or a plot-driven one, your character should travel down the path of a story arc. Along the way, the hero should learn something new. Your reader (hopefully) identifies with your hero and wants to grow as a result of spending time with your story. Your hero's transformation is reflected in your story's theme or message—an aspect of writing that many grapple with. The best way to dive into the elusive elements of theme and message is through the use of animal archetypal lessons.

For thousands of years, people have believed animals to be our spiritual helpers and guides. Many believe that if a person becomes more aware of a certain type of animal—seeing it in pictures, movies, or running into it in person—that the person should consider these awarenesses as 'divine synchronicity' and examine the energy that the animal is known for. In this way a person can consciously receive the lesson behind the animal archetype in his life, and he can move forward on his journey more easily with this lesson in mind. The lesson is, in fact, what the animal is 'trying to teach us' by coming into our lives, whether we are conscious of it or not. The animals are outward representations of an inward lesson.

WHAT IS A CHARACTER LESSON AND ARC?

In the writing of your novel or story, you want your character to go on some kind of journey, and during the journey, you want a subtle thematic message to emerge. (The masculine and feminine journeys we touched on in Part I are the focus of *45 Master Characters*. If you have read that book, I want you to know that yes, you can use these archetypal lessons with those journeys.) The ultimate arc in life is the one that leads to self-actualization. According to Maslow's hierarchy of needs, self-actualization is the result of realizing one's full potential as a human being and fulfilling a higher purpose. A great story puts a hero on a journey that contains a thematic lesson.

WHAT IS THIS 'THEME'?

Theme can be a message, a moral, a point of view, a teaching, or an insight. In fiction it is usually left unsaid and thus something the reader has to figure out for himself. When a reader discovers the theme, it gives her a feeling of satisfaction at having found a deeper purpose in a story.

It is the theme that allows the writer to connect deeply with the reader or audience. This connection is what elevates a story and makes it a classic, or makes it at least memorable.

Conversely books in which no theme exists usually upset readers. When readers don't learn anything from the experience of reading the book, a sense of emptiness results. People give up several hours of their valuable time to read a book, and they'd like to feel that they have been entertained and enlightened when they come to the end. They trust the writer to pull them out of their everyday lives for a while.

"Theme is as viable a place to begin a story as any other. When that first core competency of a story is theme, you've already got a literary tiger by the tail. Because great stories always have strong themes. But what about those who begin with theme? How does that happen, and where do those ideas come from? The answer is almost always the same—it comes from the heart. From a need to explore or proclaim a point of view about a truth, an issue, an irony or a feeling that stems from the human experience." — Larry Brooks (*Story Engineering*)

You can use animal archetypes in other ways, as the following will show, but for most of you reading this book using an animal archetype as a thematic character lesson is most appropriate.

The following examples illustrate how animals have been used in fairy tales to explore experiences, symbolize characteristics, make a point regarding relationships, and show humans crossing into extraordinary worlds. Feel free to apply the animal archetypes in this way if doing so suits your story. Once you understand the deeper meanings behind the many animal archetypes, you can craft a very interesting story using animals as heroes.

Marina Warner of *The Guardian* writes:

"The anthropologist Claude Lévi-Strauss commented that animals were "bons à penser" (good to think with), and fairytales speak through beasts to explore common experiences—fear of sexual intimacy, terror and violence and injustice, struggles for survival. A tradition of articulate, anthropomorphised creatures of every kind is as old as literature itself: animal fables and beast fairytales are found in ancient Egypt and Greece and India, and the legendary Aesop of the classics has his storytelling counterparts all over the world, who use crows and ants, lions and monkeys, ravens and donkeys to satirise the follies and vices of human beings and display along the way the effervescent cunning and high spirits of the fairytale genre." (http://www.guardian.co.uk/books/2009/oct/16/beastly-tales-warner)

I have always been drawn to animals and when I first started studying the Goddess and God archetypes for *45 Master Characters*, I came across these animal archetypes and sensed they would help with character development but was unsure how to apply them at the time.

After writing many stories of my own, I noticed that these archetypes not only worked their way into my stories, but made a great impact on them and on how people received my work. Readers seemed to really know my characters, as if the characters were very real. Readers couldn't quite say why they felt this way, but I believe it has a lot to do with the lessons embedded in my stories.

You may recognize some of the character lessons you find here, but I have presented them in a new light, by stressing their archetypal significance. While a character can find herself in countless situations (see my book *Story Structure Architect*, where I explore fifty-five of them), these archetypes illustrate deeper lessons that reach across culture and hit at a primal level. Animals are primal and instinctual, and that is why they embody the lessons so well. You can't go wrong using any of the animal archetypes because they resonate with readers on a subconscious level.

If you don't want to use these lessons for your hero in your main plot, consider using them for a supporting character in your main plot. You may also use them for your hero in your subplot.

Depending on your story, you may choose to use one lesson or several lessons. The more lessons you use, the more layers you will weave through the story. Your hero becomes more rounded by butting up against a lesson and in turn the story itself comes alive. But be careful not to overdo it.

Some of the lessons overlap a bit. This is a product of applying them to storytelling and helping you see how to use them effectively when the lesson is intangible or inwardly focused. When possible, I give examples and ways to illustrate the lesson in a dramatic way. Some lessons are so important that several animals contain some aspect of the lesson, however, a different arc takes the character through it.

Ask yourself:

- What is my hero's main goal?
- Does it include an archetypal lesson?
- If not, should it? Or should you place it in a subplot?
- Which archetypal lesson can best interfere with him reaching his goal?

- Make a list of ways you can illustrate this lesson, subtly weaving these clues to the thematic message into your story.

As far as using these animal archetypal lessons with the main archetypes found in the beginning of this book and in *45 Master Characters*: Any archetype can face any animal archetypal lesson. These lessons are for all of us. Some archetypes will naturally have learned a lesson or two and not need to face them again. There is a lot of room for creativity here.

You just have to:

- Absorb the information.
- See the possibilities.
- Take notes.
- And work out your character arc.

Remember these lessons are where a character is going, what they are learning. If you choose a lesson that is about joy, that does not mean you are writing joyful scenes for your character. It means you are challenging your character to find and learn about joy. Joy and suffering are not far apart in life.

Theme is about what the character will learn in the end. You have to get him to the end and challenge him along the way. You decide both if and how the characters get there.

SIDE NOTE:

If any of these animal archetypes conjures strong emotions for you as you read, you may want to consider that the animal you are reading about is trying to teach you a lesson on a personal level. It's impossible for me to cover all of the animal archetypal lessons here. These are the ones most applicable to writing stories.

CHAPTER 7

THE BEAR

PATIENCE & CONNECTION

"The bear is a powerful symbol and image in both myth and lore. Stories abound of individuals turned into bears, bears into humans, and bears as gods." —Ted Andrews (*Animal Speak*)

The bear uses inner resources of stored fat and the ability to shut down the kidneys to survive hibernation. Accordingly, this lesson is about learning how to sit with ideas, projects, and goals, and how to take time before moving forward. It's also about how to go with the flow while using inner resources.

Remember to let your hero dabble in the sweetness of life as well. Bears love their honey, and they feel connected to their tribe.

This lesson is about gaining control by giving up control—giving up the reactive, overly emotional way of dealing with a problem. It's not like a bear can decide not to hibernate and not to go with his natural cycles and instincts. The act of hibernating gives bears a strong sense of renewal, health, and rest. They go with their instincts and allow their bodily cycles to run their lives. In spite of what humans assume, bears are not aggressive by nature and are very loving with their young. They may be ferocious in strength but they don't want to bother much with humans. They only defend themselves if need be.

For a time I lived in the mountains of Asheville, North Carolina, where I soon discovered that bears fed from our garbage in the morning. When I saw a bear, I became quite scared. It's odd for a city person to face such a thing. But the bears didn't bother anyone—they had only stopped by for an easy snack.

THE BEAR'S CHARACTER ARC

In your story, someone may be attacking the hero, or his loved ones, on a personal level, and the hero needs to show restraint. Your hero can learn the lesson of restraint if you put him in situations where he must exhibit patience. You can use a time element that works against him. The end goal seems far off, and it looks like the hero is going to mess everything up because he can't take the time to think things through so that he can make the right decision or rest with an idea, project, or some kind of creative endeavor or business. Instead he feels the need to rush in and get things done, and doing so causes a lot of problems and conflict (which are good for the plot).

The hero is very intense and driven, almost to the point of focusing too much and in the wrong direction, simply because he didn't take the time to figure out the following:

- What he wants to do
- What he's really looking for
- What he really, really wants to achieve

Sometimes we're made to wait. Sometimes we have to refuse to believe what we are told. Sometimes we have to take time to prepare ourselves for what is to come.

Maybe the hero wants to be on a soccer team but doesn't make the cut. His only choice is to take the time to develop the necessary skills. He must train in order to become a better player. Getting on the team is his goal. It's all about being patient and taking the time to see new options and opportunities.

It's human nature to want to hurry up and get to 'the end' (I know a lot of my writer friends want to), and many people don't care how they get there. They want things done so they can move on to the next thing. As a result, they shoot themselves in the foot because they're not taking the time necessary to consider all of the available options and complete their task in a way that will bring them closer to their goal and help them out in other areas of life.

When you are making decisions—especially decisions made at the level a hero makes them—there are many things to consider, and this is where the conflict comes in this lesson.

- He is not hibernating.
- He is not taking his time.
- He is not finding patience.
- He is not finding different options and opportunities.
- Villainous characters may be trying to use his emotions against him.

He may possess intense power and energy, but he doesn't need to be aggressive in applying it. He needs to see the value in what other people can contribute, and he needs to take the time to stop and look and see other ways of doing things in order to be successful.

Your plot must be somewhat complex so your heroine is forced to consider many options.

This lesson teaches the heroine how to slow down, how to go with what life is throwing at her, how not to jump to the wrong conclusions. Very often a person switches to autopilot, meaning she stops seeing things as they actually are. If she's experienced certain difficulties in life and similar situations present themselves to her, she will go through the databank in her mind and apply what has happened in the past to what's happening at present. Very often this is not a good thing. She ends up making assumptions, and she jumps to conclusions, and may go off in the wrong direction. By being in the reactive mind, she may ruin relationships. Reacting to events without thinking or seeing the bigger picture can result in a dire situation.

A character can move in the wrong directions and generally screw himself up on false assumptions and by not seeing a clear picture of what's actually happening in front of him. He gets so involved in his own drama and process and pain that he may not consider that maybe, for example, his girlfriend is canceling on him not because she has found a new boyfriend but because she is sick or some type of tragedy has occurred.

He jumps to conclusions that she is with another man because of things that have happened in his past. This can happen in business too. For example, a prospective client saying no to the hero's proposal makes the hero think his prices are too high. Actually the client is telling the truth when he says he needs to delay the project until funds are available. This is different from a misunderstanding; it's the hero's misinterpretation of a situation, or his rushing to make a decision just because he want to cross a task off his list.

STORY EXAMPLES

Rain Man

The materialistic Tom Cruise character initially kidnaps his brother from a facility and holds him for ransom, which is half the inheritance his father left solely to his unknown brother, Dustin Hoffman. As Cruise learns to love his brother, he decides that his brother is more important to him than the money he demanded. Every step of the way he must learn to have patience with his brother.

King Lear

Once Lear is driven to the end of his rope, he cries out at the cruelties of Goneril and Regan. *"You heavens, give me that patience, patience I need!"* King Lear cannot approach his situation or obtain his goal without learning how to have patience. As you can see, this is not the plot but part of the theme.

This lesson works very well with the Mystery genre too. The hero needs to take time to reflect and consider facts and behavior in order to get the big picture and solve the mystery.

WHY MIGHT YOUR HERO RESIST THIS LESSON?

A hero would resist this kind of lesson because it's his nature to want to get things done quickly. There is a reason, which can be found in his past, for why he is so compelled to get things done quickly, to rush into assumptions, to get into reactive mode, and therefore to make the wrong decisions and choices.

He may feel like he's the boss and anything he says should be law. Why should he have to worry about controlling his emotions and passions? If he wants to move forward, he's going to do what he wants to do when he wants to do it.

In general, it's really hard to slow down; most people don't want to slow down because when they exercise patience and do actually slow down, many of the reasons behind why they are so busy and frantic come to the surface. These reasons are things they don't want to face or think about. So the busier they are and the faster they are moving through life, the less time they have to face these things.

Something in the character's history makes him want to run away. That's something you'll need to figure out. What happened? What incident occurred when he was thirteen years old that is pushing this character and giving him such drive, even though that drive is causing him to make all kinds of mistakes and create his own conflict? This character does a really good job of creating the conflict more than any villain could.

HOW DO OTHER CHARACTERS VIEW THIS LESSON?

Supporting characters may feel that this lesson is imperative to the hero. Usually heroes who have been very intensely rushing through life cause 'collateral damage' for their supporting characters. Each time the hero suffers another dilemma, the supporting characters help him pick up the pieces. So the supporters might be happy, perhaps to a smug degree, to watch the hero learn this lesson. They may support him wholeheartedly, or they may do their best to help him avoid the lesson for their own personal gain. It, of course, depends on their relationship.

People who are in a subordinate position at work may have no choice but to help him in his pursuits. They have to do what he says even if they see that he's moving in a useless direction.

SUCCESSFUL RESOLUTION

In a successful resolution the hero will learn:

- How to have patience
- How to stop and understand when he is jumping into reactive mode and making assumptions
- How to deal with people in a more relaxed way
- To really see and listen to what's happening around him
- To really think about what he is doing before he does it
- To look at long-term consequences of decisions and actions

A successful outcome will include the hero's inner healing and a new ability to make a more balanced, grounded decision that will take him to his goal.

TRAGIC RESOLUTION

In an unsuccessful resolution, the hero doesn't understand where he goes wrong. Even if he starts to understand at some point in the story, in the end he rushes to a decision or assumption that puts the goal out of his reach—and maybe into the hands of someone who was more patient.

HOW CAN YOU ILLUSTRATE THIS LESSON?

You can use bears to symbolically show hibernation, of course, but it's always best to consider the props that will best suit your setting. For instance, in this example, you might infuse meditative, Zen-like qualities into certain settings in your story. The hero's place will not be meditative, but some of the places the hero goes might be.

You can also suggest these qualities through the mood and tone of a scene. For instance, the hero's dialogue can be very, very short and choppy. He may use words that are fast and phonetic and frantic, to reflect his life's fast, fast pace.

Juxtapose the hero's choppy dialogue with longer passages and flowery verbiage to show the opposite, more patient alternative. A love interest could mirror the hero's fast-paced way by being very patient and also by giving him the benefit of the doubt. Or his love interest may be jumping to a conclusion against him and he finds himself confused wondering, "what the hell happened?" He starts seeing what its like to be on the receiving end of this kind of stuff.

The hero's impatience can appear in the subtext of the dialogue. Things may be left unsaid because he's in such a hurry to move on. Similarly, the character might be moving around the room, rushing here to there, picking up objects, and grabbing items and rearranging them to show his constant movement.

In the subplot, you might show another character who is trying to make a decision and can't make one. Or you might have characters near to this character impatiently wondering *"Did he decide yet, did he make a decision?!"*

Somebody else at work might be going crazy waiting for the boss (hero) to make a decision. Or, it could be the hero's best friend who needs to make a decision—maybe he is getting married and cannot decide what color the groomsman's cummerbund should be and the inability to make such a small decision just drives the hero crazy. That's one way of showing it.

With this kind of lesson, you will need a positive influence to demonstrate the benefits of patience and hibernation, and how these benefits don't sap a person's strength. The hero can meet someone who is patient. He needs to watch someone else retain their strength, without aggressiveness and without rushing and bullying their way through problems. Possessing that power in a way that is more balanced and more useful to him will allow him to make grounded, useful decisions.

TWISTS

This universal lesson, which crosses all genders and cultures, allows for many twists. For instance, consider an area in the hero's life where he does exhibit patience. It might be a quirky hobby such as building ships in a bottle. Such a deviation would make an interesting twist in his personality. It shows that he does have the skill to focus and take the necessary time to be precise and think ahead. It also hints that he potentially could turn his problems around. You might create an instance in which he has to make a really quick decision. He is the only person in the room who can make the decision, and he winds up saving the day.

These are just some of the ways you can use this lesson to add conflict and interesting facets to the hero in your story. As you can see, you can definitely make this lesson the main theme of your story.

AUDIENCE INTEREST

Hibernation is universal and therefore a lot of people can relate to it. Readers will enjoy watching how your heroine grapples with her problems and hopefully comes out ahead.

Meditation and relaxation techniques exist in part to get people out of their reactive mind-set. In other words, to stop them from jumping to conclusions and offer an alternative to staying constantly busy. Most people can relate to how hard it is to sit in silence and deal with the many thoughts that come bubbling up as you relax and get more grounded. That's why this is a lesson that a lot of readers will relate to—and that's good because you want to use lessons in your story that people can identify with.

THE BUFFALO

GRATITUDE & TRUST

> "A Buffalo's hump occurs at shoulder level, this implies that we must incorporate our own efforts. Shoulders are symbols of the ability to embrace and hold life…and our burdens or rewards. Afterall 'The Lord helps those who help themselves'"
> —Ted Andrews (*Animal Speak*)

Buffalos have very humped shoulders and horns, indicating a shored-up sense of power, strength, and stamina. They are very strong and protective, yet somewhat noble and graceful. At the same time, their skins and meat have clothed, fed, and provided shelter to native peoples for so many years. Native Indians saw buffalos as an abundant source of life and were grateful and respectful of this animal's presence on earth.

I remember traveling across the United States once and stopping at a park where buffalos hang out on the other side of a short wooden log fence. I was so in awe of their size and beauty, I didn't make it back to the trailer in time, and my friends took off without me. Alone with the buffalos, I noticed how they graze in a group, respectful of each other, communicating with body language and receiving the abundance around them. (By the way: My friends did notice I was missing and came back for me.)

The lesson here is to learn how to be grateful for what you have and for what's around you, and to recognize the abundance you have in your life so you can welcome more of it in. If you are not grateful for what you have, and you focus only on what you're lacking, the people around you will not be quick to help you because you don't respect or value what you already have. Why would the universe give you more to be ungrateful for?

You must respect the people around you, the resources around you, and the job that you have, even if you hate doing it. Your job deserves a certain amount of gratitude and respect because it is there for you if you need it. You can walk away from your job, if you really want to. Maybe you won't be able to pay your rent, but you won't cease to exist.

The following basic rules can apply to any area of life: Be grateful for what you have, see and respect the abundance around you, and trust that things will work out. It is spiritual and divine to know and trust that the universe will provide for you.

A note here: Inspirational stories fall into this lesson category. Sometimes they feel predictable because readers know going in that the hero will succeed. It's important, therefore, to make the story about the path the hero takes and not only about the successful ending.

THE BUFFALO'S CHARACTER ARC

Cynicism, pessimism, and self-deprecation are signs of shame and self-punishment. They are not noble qualities and they do not result from realistic thinking, as many would believe. So you can have a hero that is cynical and pessimistic, and furthermore, ungrateful and disrespectful of what she has. She cannot see the abundance around her nor does she trust that things will work out. She is full of shame and self-punishment, and does not feel like she deserves anything good, let alone great.

This definitely fits a character-driven story well. The character could start out feeling like she is at a low point in her life, only to find that things got a lot lower later on and that her life wasn't as bad as she thought at that time. She realizes that she should have been grateful for what she had.

This can also work for a romantic relationship: Maybe the heroine doesn't appreciate her partner, and then her partner is gone and she realizes she didn't respect the relationship or the person, and she wasn't grateful for the things that he did for her. She didn't see the abundant love and possibility that was right in front of her. She didn't trust that things could get better if she had worked on them. It's the old saying about not realizing what you have until it's gone.

Her friends could be out seizing opportunities and she could be pushed away by being so negative about every step that they are taking to the point where they don't want to be around her anymore.

STORY EXAMPLES

Eat, Pray, Love
After her divorce, the Julia Roberts character embarks on a spiritual journey of indulgence (Italy), prayer (India), and balance (Bali), and she learns to receive abundance and be grateful for what she has.

The Pursuit of Happyness
This is the true-life story of a single dad who tries to build a better life for him and his son. His son must trust him along the way, and the hero shows gratitude every step of the way. *"I'm grateful for the chance,"* he says. Nothing stands in his way as an obstacle. Since the story plays out as a flashback, we know the hero is successful in the end, but we still want to see how he did it.

It's a Wonderful Life
George Bailey recognizes his life as wonderful, only after suffering many hardships, and learning the value of trusting and helping others. People do come to help him when he needs them.

The Blind Side
Everyone is grateful in this true story of a wealthy woman who mentors a homeless boy.

WHY YOUR CHARACTER MIGHT RESIST THIS LESSON

Conflict occurs when the hero pushes away what little she possesses. It also occurs when she overlooks opportunities and forgoes chances that seem insignificant to her at that time.

It can also come from the heroine's hopeless feelings. *"Why should I even bother?"* she thinks. She is looking at everything in her life in a cynical and pessimistic way. When she says *"That's just the way it is,"* and accepts her horrible fate, she believes she is being realistic about life.

If she were to see the blessings around her, and recognize and respect all the things she should be grateful for, her identity as the cynical, pessimistic gal who thinks she is realistic would shatter. She doesn't want to lose her identity, so she will fight to keep things the way they are. She may be somewhat happy to be known as the Cynic, thinking, *"Well, I'm realistic and I can see that coming a mile away. Nobody is going to get anything on me."*

HOW DO OTHER CHARACTERS VIEW THIS LESSON?

Supporting characters would encourage her to see the value of what she has. A lot of them probably have tried to make her see, but only a harsh wake-up call will do the trick. She needs to learn how to count her blessings, to put things in perspective, to understand that her view of life as cynical and pessimistic is skewed and a symptom of not caring for and respecting herself.

She may not take very good care of herself at all. She may be smoking too much and develop emphysema. Her house may be a mess. She may be running, running, running like the George Clooney character who constantly travels in the movie *Up in the Air*.

SUCCESSFUL RESOLUTION

In a successful resolution, the heroine will learn the lesson without having to go through too much pain or loneliness, without having to completely bottom out. That might be the ultimate version of success, but it wouldn't be very dramatic. Instead, your heroine should hit bottom in some area of her life. Something significant should happen that provides a wake-up call and forces her to count her blessings. Then she can be successful in hearing that call.

TRAGIC RESOLUTION

In a tragic resolution, the heroine doesn't get the lesson and messes up her life to the point that her goal cannot be achieved and her circumstances cannot be repaired. She must let go and move on. In an alternative version, she can learn the lesson in the end but she isn't going to achieve her goal and in the meantime her whole life has changed. She learns the lesson, but it's too late.

HOW CAN YOU ILLUSTRATE THIS LESSON?

Symbols of abundance and gratitude, and a love of life can appear in the mood and tone. You can juxtapose dark and light scenes, sunny or rainy days, dingy or super-clean locations. The heroine's apartment may be a cluttered mess, and she might partake in bad habits and you can include props that hint at how she spends her time.

Consider letting the facial expressions (subtext) of other characters impart the effect she has on the outside world. When she is talking to a friend, for instance, you might show that person's telling look of pity or dissatisfaction as they listen to what she says.

Other characters could illustrate the need to learn a similar lesson. Maybe a wealthy character in the subplot remains unsatisfied, though he has an abundance of money. Perhaps this guy isn't grateful for what he has because he knows everything can be taken away from him at anytime. The heroine might look down on this character, thinking, *"What's the matter with him? If I had those millions I would be doing great..."* She does not see the parallel to her own life.

TWISTS

You can make your story more interesting by adding some twists to this lesson. You might include in your plotline a person who has absolutely nothing and yet is happy and grateful to be alive. Another idea is to include a character who is very wealthy and also very grateful, respectful, and happy giving much of her money away. She gives to charities and then visits those organizations and sees what good her money has done. She feels blessed to be able to help these people. Play with this idea and see where it takes you.

AUDIENCE INTEREST

This lesson draws a lot of interest because so many of us know a person (or people) who is cynical despite having much to be grateful for. We may even be that person, or if not, we have at least experienced a moment during which we felt this kind of cynicism. We may not want to admit to our cynicism, but we do like to think we are blessed more than we know and we need only to look a little deeper to see it.

It's a Wonderful Life is such a popular classic because we can relate to sometimes feeling really bad about what's going on in our lives until we meet somebody who is worse off than ourselves. It's a universal lesson.

CHAPTER 9

THE COUGAR

ASSERTIVENESS & MASTERY

"Often times, Cougar 'people' face issues and examples of what true power is and what it isn't. True power is never about trying to have power over someone else. Power and owning one's power means one accepts responsibility for one's choices and actions, one accepts that every action one takes leads to consequences that may be positive or negative.
—Lynx Graywolf

Cougars are very good at using their resources. They only move when they are sure it's a good time to take action. They watch and study what's going on around them and wait for the right time to make a move. They don't waste a lot of energy and time in the faulty pursuits or in moves in the wrong direction.

They know what needs to be done. They've figured everything out ahead of time. They have weighed their options, and they are ready to make a move. They are waiting for that right moment to come, and they will pounce on that opportunity.

This lesson is about a focused, readied, skilled, knowledgeable attack. It is similar to going to war—the troops are just waiting for their superiors to give the go-ahead so they can move forward. It's about the external part of getting ready to react because everything is aligned and ready to go. They're just waiting for the opportunity.

The hero in this case is starting from a place of power. He may be getting bullied but he already has within him the strength to deal with it. He just may need a little push in asserting himself.

Assertiveness is about being centered in what you know is best and speaking up. It is not about being a bully or pushing your weight around. It's about having confidence and doing what you think is right in the situation you are facing.

THE COUGAR'S CHARACTER ARC

The entire story can be about the hero getting ready for the SOMETHING moment. Viewers watch him becoming assertive; stepping into his power and space, becoming knowledgeable. He is figuring out who he is and what his skills are, and really getting to know himself and what he offers.

Or it can be about a character who already knows himself and is already prepared, but for one reason or another is allowing another character (or an area of his life) to wreck his plan. He has to deal with those issues before he can step up.

He is ready to pounce, but something happens to stop him. For example, a business merger is his top priority but then his mother or spouse gets sick or has a crisis situation and needs his attention. The story becomes a question of priorities and about learning a life lesson. It's about the hero knowing who he is and where he should focus his assertiveness. An assertive character would likely go to the hospital and really get on top of his spouse's medical treatment and make sure everything is running smoothly.

You could also apply the hero's assertive behavior in places where it's not going to do much good. The hero needs to learn that sometimes he needs to step back and assert his power in more subtle ways. More often than not, a conflict arises when the hero abuses his power or gets his priorities mixed up. This is a second kind of hero that really is not assertive and desperately needs to learn to be in order to reach his goal.

STORY EXAMPLES:

Office Space
The hero decides he's not going to be a corporate drone and stands up to the bosses (asserting himself), which winds up getting him a promotion. He decides he doesn't want to work at all anymore and hatches a plan to steal money from the corporation.

Lord of the Flies by William Golding
Ralph pushed Piggy to one side. "I was chief, and you were going to do what I said." Ralph learns to assert his power, but he does so for the sake of the signal fire and to help everyone get rescued. He sees power rightly used in the right time or the right reason.

The Matrix
Neo must learn to embrace his talents and skills, but they are of no use if he cannot assert his power and stand up for himself. He becomes not only the master of his life, but the master of the entire matrix. He develops a plan to save Morpheus and executes it against the advice of others.

WHY MIGHT YOUR CHARACTER RESIST THIS LESSON?
Whether the hero has the necessary zeal to take this on or not, this lesson is life-changing. It's life-changing to become assertive and to analyze your priorities and determine how well you are handling them. The internal drive to achieve these things is necessary and may be enough to make a change, but the hero will face pressure from the outside world to stay the course and not be assertive. Even if he is being assertive and going for that opportunity, other characters may not want to see that opportunity happen for him. If the hero does not want to disappoint people, he may have trouble being assertive.

Here are some other reasons your character might resist this lesson:

- We like to please others, which is not very assertive.
- We like to be a part of the group and part of the team.
- We like to be accepted and valued.
- We don't want to lose our friends and feel alone and abandoned. We want to be accepted and included by our peers.

HOW DO OTHER CHARACTERS VIEW THIS LESSON?

Other characters usually support the right use of assertiveness and power, as well as good decision making and the seizing of opportunities. It's a question of who the character is to the hero. Usually one area of the hero's life, whether it's work or family, is going to suffer in order for him to become an assertive leader who is focused and ready for opportunity. To create drama and conflict, you can have ancillary events occur and mess things up so the hero misses opportunities.

For this hero, being assertive means using his strengths in a healthy way. It's not aggressive, though other characters may see it that way and accuse him of doing something bad. The hero's newfound assertiveness will change the dynamic between him and his friends. That's why this is a powerful lesson to learn—an outwardly focused lesson. The hero may need to learn how to be more assertive or how to juggle priorities and have balance in life.

SUCCESSFUL RESOLUTION

A successful resolution occurs when the character is able to develop assertiveness and the appropriate use of power, or when he finds a way to balance in his life. He meets his goal in the end by retaining his assertiveness and power while figuring out a way to manage all the little bumps that have come between him and his goal.

TRAGIC RESOLUTION

An unsuccessful resolution occurs when the hero uses his assertiveness in an aggressive way. He is pushed to his limits and unable to stand in a balanced assertive way. He gets a little too aggressive and sets his priorities in the wrong place. In the case of the character who needs to develop assertiveness, he backslides and winds up helping someone else to be more assertive.

In the end, this character has failed in one sense. But maybe this task was not the whole story. Learning this lesson might be a subplot or a character arc within a much larger arc. Maybe the character was not able to become assertive; instead he becomes accepting of himself: *"Look, this is how I am, and I don't feel comfortable with being that assertive. It's just not me and I'm okay with that."* That's an in-between kind of outcome, which is fine.

There are no real "have-tos" in life. A wrong use of power and assertiveness often leads to a tragic resolution for the character.

HOW CAN YOU ILLUSTRATE THIS LESSON?

How would you show this? You could have a very natural, instinctual, safari kind of setting. Conversely props and costumes can be very sharp and calculated, and everything must have a reason for being there. Nothing is superfluous or flamboyant; think very structured, useful, and practical. The setting, props, and costuming all have that same mood, tone, and theme. A sense of sharpness prevails.

Time can be an element in this story. It's the usual passing time but in a way that is assertive and powerful and almost corporate.

TWISTS

You can use gender as a way to give this lesson a twist because it is "not as acceptable" for women to be assertive as it is for men. Women may have to give up certain areas of their lives because it's hard to be assertive all day in the workplace and to revert to feminine energy for relationships. A lot of professionals find they have to learn how to switch gears.

Play around with this gender and have a male character that must learn to be assertive. That could make him feel better in his masculinity since he is not that way now. Another man could be making fun of him. You could also use a cultural twist. Many cultures portray men as more assertive than women. You could definitely play with that stereotype by making the man in the story less assertive and the woman more assertive. He constantly needs a secretary to step up and take care of business.

Observe people in their daily lives. You will see that often people who aren't assertive at all will become very assertive when a situation involves standing up for their kids or their pets. They are more willing to become assertive for loved ones than for themselves.

Some people mistake anger for assertiveness. Anger is not the same thing as assertiveness and many people need to learn this lesson. Yelling and being mean, hurtful, and angry is not assertive behavior. That's another twist you might want to use. Perhaps some character thinks he's being assertive, but he's not.

It's an interesting lesson to play with, one that offers the opportunity to experiment with different character dynamics and varying positions and levels of power, especially within companies. Other areas of life can throw a wrench in the works while your hero waits for his opportunity and prepares for his moment to pounce.

AUDIENCE INTEREST

Everyone has moments where they wish they had been more assertive. It's like the *Seinfeld* episode, when George was made fun of in a meeting and afterwards thought, *"Oh, I should have said 'Yeah? Well the Jerkstore called and they were running out of you.'"*

A lot of us feel like we would have been more successful in life had we been more assertive, had we been ready for opportunities, had we been more calculated and prepared. We wish we did not let other areas of our life stop us, and we wish we did not let fear stop us. Many readers will relate to such a story arch.

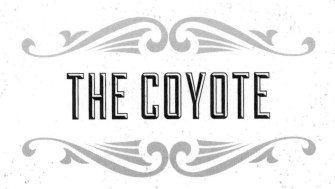

CHAPTER 10

THE COYOTE

CURIOSITY & RESOURCEFULNESS

"If a Coyote totem has appeared in your life, be prepared for Murphy's Law to enter your life with a vengeance. Your sense of humor will need to arise full force in keeping with the things happening around you." LinsDomain.com

Back in 2006 a coyote found his fifteen minutes of fame when he made his way to Central Park and wandered the park for two days. And then in 2007 a coyote entered a busy restaurant in the Chicago Loop district. These incidents are great examples of the coyote's curious and adventurous nature, as well as their ability to adapt to their surroundings.

Coyotes know how to survive and adapt with a sense of adventurous curiosity and play. It is amazing to note that thousands of them live in cities without having contact with humans. These tricksters break the rules and live life on their own terms.

Life can be miserable if we merely endure it and are constantly involved in the pain, suffering, and mishaps that are bound to happen (at least until one has reached a higher level of awareness). In any moment of any day, drama abounds if you look for it.

The best way to deal with the struggles of life is to learn to laugh at yourself and to do some foolish things once in a while to lighten the mood. You need to relax and indulge in a bit of silly adventurousness once in a while. In your old age, you will want some crazy memories to look back on.

THE COYOTE'S CHARACTER ARC

It is interesting to see a story that is about getting to a place of foolishness, where you can laugh at yourself and indulge in your playful side. We have seen the inventive and resourceful side of this lesson portrayed in stories quite a bit. For instance, many stories show characters who need to face breaking the rules in order to do the right thing and save the day.

A lot of kids' stories incorporate this element of 'loosening up' because kids like to see adults act more like children. The coyote trickster character can be the catalyst that changes the adult while the children remain untouched.

Many laugh quite a bit watching *The Hangover*, whose cast includes an anal-retentive dentist who loosens up to the point of marrying a stripper and losing one of his teeth. The consequences that the friends face are hilarious, but in the end they need to tone down their crazy ways. They almost went too far and got punished for it.

STORY EXAMPLES

Groundhog Day

An arrogant weather forecaster is annoyed when he finds himself stuck in Punxsutawney, Pennsylvania, due to a snowstorm. He goes to bed and wakes up only to repeat the same day over and over again. He does everything he can to try to get out of his predicament but finally accepts his fate and does the best he can with it, learning to help others and try to make things better for all so he can repeat a better day over and over again.

The Hangover

A group of guys head to Vegas for a bachelor party. They wind up getting into the most outrageous trouble imaginable in order to try to find the groom when no one can remember what happened the night before. They face so many trials and feel like giving up but in many scenes they laugh at themselves and press on, not letting the intense panic and fear they each feel inside get them down or distract them from the task at hand. In fact, they go a bit too far and are punished for it.

Bridges of Madison County by Robert James Waller

Photographer Robert Kincaid wanders into the life of housewife Francesca Johnson for four days in the 1960s. Her family is away, and she must decide if she will give up everything for love (see Tragic resolution below).

Arthur

Russell Brand's character, Arthur, is out to have fun at all costs. Hobson (his nanny) enables his behavior. She enjoys the excitement and drama he brings to her life. She supports his foolishness in her actions while her words contradict what she does. If any hardship comes his way, he throws money and booze at it. He will not endure any of the pain of life. He takes pride in acting a fool and is willing to act stupid so other people will do things for him. When Hobson gets sick and passes away, Arthur has no choice but to grow up. His story moves in the opposite direction of most, from unsustainable foolishness to responsible foolishness. In the end he maintains that spark of innocence and love of life.

ET

An alien, stranded on earth, befriends a group of kids who try to help him get home. The little sister, Gertie, provides comic relief. She is a trickster who causes trouble and threatens to tell mom what is going on. She really just wants to be included.

WHY MIGHT YOUR CHARACTER RESIST THIS LESSON

The heroine may resist her foolish, playful side because she is afraid of what might happen if she drops her serious side. Will her house of cards crumble?

Deep inside she may be a fun extrovert, but she is afraid if she lets go and does something foolish, something horrible may happen. She's afraid she will not be able to get back to the responsible person she was. If she loosens up and lets her guard down, she may experience too much of a release. For some people, it's really hard to let loose.

Some people try to spice up their lives in little ways. They test the water with something small and may leave it at that. But other characters can't do even that much. Their idea of crazy may be to let the pictures fall to one side without setting them right again. Think of the character Niles in *Frasier*.

If the hero jumps in, she will have fun. She will experience a renewal and invite energy into her life.

I often tell people, writers especially, to go out and have an adventure. That is the best way to get over writer's block. Completely distracting your mind with fun and laughter allows a refreshed energy into your life. A bit of fear may come with the responsibility of this new energy, as well as the shift in life that occurs when one lets go.

Perhaps a character's doctor tells him that he has to stop being so angry and negative and depressed. His doctor suggests: *"Write down your thoughts and see how many negative ones you are having about every little thing that happens. Then you will see that you are stressing yourself out. It's bad for your heart and it's bad for your soul."*

HOW DO OTHER CHARACTERS VIEW THIS LESSON?

A lot of other characters would support the hero in learning this lesson unless they are heavily invested in being responsible and proper.

Deep down, everybody wants to laugh and joke around, even in the worst of times. When hard times hit, and life is just too heavy and too much, everyone is grateful for a class clown who says something silly and lightens the mood.

Artistic characters are the kind who may want to delve deeper into their silly sides in an effort to see things differently. They tend to be overly intense in their pursuits, so that could be interesting to watch.

Here the hero needs to obtain the following skills:

- The ability to stop in the moment of pain, suffering, or despair or just a mishap
- The ability to step back
- The ability to see the bigger picture
- The ability to find something funny in the situation

TRAGIC RESOLUTION

A tragic resolution occurs when the heroine does not go far enough. She starts her pursuit, meets resistance, and stops cold. Or the heroine gets there and thinks that it's just too much for her, she just can't shake her negative thinking. Perhaps there is a bit of this at the end in *Bridges of Madison County,* when Francesca can't open the car door and jump into the adventurous life she really wants with a new man. She feels the call of duty to stay with her family but perhaps she is afraid of taking a risk. Maybe everyday life would kill the romance they had, and she's better off living with her memories.

SUCCESSFUL RESOLUTION

A successful resolution occurs when the heroine embraces her foolish side and loosens up. It might be funny to watch how the dramatic events of life try to stop her, but she still wants to have fun and keeps trying. In the end she is able to integrate this lesson because she decides that it doesn't matter what happens, that she will find the fun in all of it.

HOW CAN YOU ILLUSTRATE THIS LESSON?

Life can be painful and you may want to portray your characters as beaten down. You can show this through symbols, setting, and costuming. A trickster or shape-shifter character works well here. Shape-shifters have always been associated with the coyote's Murphy's Law ways of wreaking a zany form of havoc in people's lives to teach them lessons.

The effects of this kind of transformational arc could be present in the setting. Think lots of color versus bland beiges. The character might change her way of dress, from a pared-down, simple style into more flowery, colorful, vibrant outfits. Perhaps those around her wonder "What's *changed about her?"* They recognize a difference. The way the characters react to her might be comical, prompting the heroine to think, *"Oh my god, all I did was change my shirt, people, calm down!"* Indications can even occur in the dialogue. All of a sudden, the hero is using words she never used before: *"Well, I have been broadening my vocabulary,"* she says.

You can also be innovative and resourceful in a different way that isn't about laughter and comedy but is more about taking risks. In more serious films, you can have the hero take risks that get more and more crazy.

TWISTS

Some cultures don't value risk taking and indulging in playfulness or being inventive. They value responsibility and the act of sacrificing for the group. These are things the hero will come up against.

The hero may make the decision to be 100 percent onboard. Just then events of life occur that challenge this decision, making for hilarious twists in themselves.

In an action movie, the heroine might be ready to start taking risks and suddenly a risk she has to take presents itself and it's through the roof. This lesson is a great way to add some comedy into a story.

AUDIENCE INTEREST

Many people are familiar with the fear of change. Changing one's outlook on life is a scary prospect. But many of us want to do it in an effort to be happier. We all want joy in our lives. We all want to better deal with the pain in our lives. Most of the time, we just can't figure out how to do it.

Many of us believe that having certain things, or striving for perfection, or achieving knowledge will save us. When those things don't work, some people look to pills or doctors to save them. They don't realize that they need to save themselves, that they need to change their outlook on life. Living the moment in a different way may be the answer. Most people would be very interested to see how a heroine navigates through such waters.

CHAPTER 11

THE DEER

INNOCENCE & AWARENESS

"Deer is a keen observer, enabled to see well in low lighting and its sensitive hearing allows it to perceive a twig snap in the distance. Deer is a messenger of serenity, can see between shadows and hear what isn't being said. Deer teaches us to maintain our innocence and gentleness so we can share our open-heartedness with others." Animaltotem.com

When you see a deer, it's hard not to notice how graceful and sensitive it is. Deer can hear the rustle of leaves under footsteps from very far away. They are able to perceive the type of animal that's coming closer. They are always aware and observant of what's going on around them because they are, after all, prey.

They need to be keenly observant and intuitive. They have the appearance of grace, sensitivity, caring, and going with the flow.

The deer teaches observers to hear what isn't being said, that is, to read between the lines or hear below the surface. The deer demonstrates how to get an understanding of things that are not spoken, not demonstrated, and not brought to one's attention.

In order to survive, they can't be deep in their own minds, preoccupied with things that don't concern with what's going on around them. They have to pay attention, they must be present.

With most animals, some special awareness remains ever present, even in the playful times or when eating. Deer don't have much in the way of protecting themselves (though males have antlers, they are only hard enough to use during the fall and early winter), but they do have gifts of instinct, intuition, and keen hearing. All of these things help them survive. As a group, its their Plan B. They always make sure they know a way out.

This lesson is about maintaining your innocence regardless of what circumstances you are facing. It's about maintaining your inner spark throughout your life, rather than allowing what happens to harden you. (*Citizen Kane* is a great example of what happens when a person fails at this.)

It's about seeing why things have happened the way they have and not giving up. It's about dealing with things in an unusual way so that we don't turn into the oppressor. The goals are to maintain your sense of self, that childlike (not *childish*) innocence and gentleness toward life and to always have a plan B in place to protect yourself.

I once went deer hunting with a bow and arrow. I didn't know much about arrows or hunting but a friend invited me and I enjoy nature so I went. I remember sitting in the woods for hours, literally. I merely sat there in the quiet. I was unable to move because my friend was hunting and I couldn't ruin things for him by making noise. It was very Zen-like to sit in complete silence, listening for that first snap of a twig, waiting and waiting. I was learning how to be aware of my surroundings. This is how deer live.

My friend didn't shoot at anything that day, and I was so relieved—I'd rather look for deer and interact with them. Later he said he just goes for the quiet.

THE DEER'S CHARACTER ARC

For the character arc, the hero might need to live more in the present, even if it's just in order to negotiate a business deal.

The hero needs to:

- Be more aware of what is not being said
- Know what people may be doing in the periphery
- Hear what's going on below the surface
- See what's coming before it happens
- Be able to plan for different options
- Have a plan B ready at all times

He must learn his lesson in a way that is not fanatical, radical, obsessive, or fearful. Show it in a very calm sort of way.

You could have a hero who is more tyrannical and fearful, and always looking for the next bad thing to happen to him. This is prey-like, in that he is waiting for something or someone to come along and possibly do him harm. But then he starts to understand that he can plan. He can foresee a lot of things. He can calm down and use his intuition and his gut, and at some point he just has to let go and trust that he will be able to observe and protect himself if necessary. He will not allow fear to change him or push him into a bad decision.

STORY EXAMPLES:

ET

An alien, stranded on earth, befriends a group of kids who try to help him get home. ET is an innocent character that never lets go of his loving ways, no matter what the people on earth do to him. He is a bit jumpy and very aware of what is going on around him. He quickly develops a plan B to get home.

The Catcher in the Rye by J.D. Salinger

Holden is afraid of growing up and would prefer to remain an innocent child. He flunks many classes at school. *"They kicked me out. I wasn't sup-*

pose to come back after Christmas vacation, on account of I was flunking four subjects and not applying myself at all." The novel deals with adolescent issues. Retaining one's innocence is a major focus.

Citizen Kane

This story is about the loss of innocence. "Rosebud" is used to push the story forward and to impart the theme at the same time, for it represents this high-powered man's life and is the word he utters at death when the story opens. Throughout the movie, we want to know what Rosebud refers to.

British Romantic Literature focuses heavily on innocence, employing the child and the savage as main characters. Innocence is seen as the way to spirituality.

WHY MIGHT YOUR CHARACTER RESIST THIS LESSON?

A character might resist this lesson because although people feel instinctively with their guts, they are taught to value only what can be seen and heard directly. Protecting oneself via what one sees and hears usually does not turn out well, but time and again we are taught to value facts over intuition.

As we grow up, we give up our innocence and generosity, and become hardened. We often live in fear and look out for who might hurt us or attack us. In this way, we live outside of the present moment. We think that somehow living this way is smarter than dealing with the present and that it will somehow protect us. Everyone around us supports this idea.

People may also resist the idea of trying to retain their innocence. They feel that being childlike is childish, though there is a big difference between the two.

HOW DO OTHER CHARACTERS VIEW THIS LESSON?

Other characters might be put off by this lesson because it's hard for anybody in modern society to keep their innocence and generosity, especially those who live in the city. City folks assume that people who let their guard down are simply asking someone to take advantage of them.

It's possible to remain aware and stay true to who you are in spite of what happens around you. You can continue to be somewhat innocent and gentle, but you'll need to protect yourself. That means staying attuned to what's going on around you in the present moment, hearing what's not being said, and using your peripheral vision so you can be aware of your surroundings.

It's not about being on alert or being hypervigilant. The aim is to achieve a relaxing presence that honors your gut instincts and intuition, and does not allow whatever is going on around you to change the core of who you are. Many of us struggle with this.

A story of a Zen student illustrates this lesson well. The Zen student is being harassed by a man on the street. One day she takes her umbrella and hits him over the head. Then she notices that her Zen teacher is watching from across the street. She apologizes to the teacher and asks what she should do about the situation. He replies, "Next time, gather a lot of love in your heart and hit him over the head." This means that if you have the right intention when defending yourself, it is acceptable to do whatever you see fit. The teacher goes on to say that the man who harassed the student also needs a lesson.

SUCCESSFUL RESOLUTION

A successful outcome occurs when the hero learns how to balance both sides and walk that middle ground to ensure he keeps his generosity, gentleness, and innocence intact. He is grounded and aware so he can stay protected and be present, and therefore handle anything that may come up. A lot of self-trust is involved in living this way. The character may face many tests.

TRAGIC RESOLUTION

A tragic outcome occurs when the hero can't let go of the anger, fear, and belief that people are out to get him. These things are too great a part of who he is. He's afraid that if he allows an innocence and gentleness into his life, he may be completely destroyed. He simply won't feel safe.

HOW CAN YOU ILLUSTRATE THIS LESSON?

You can show the hero being tested, and you can have him use or not use his intuitive senses and gut feelings to get through each test. As far as symbols go, consider incorporating things that in some ways portray innocence. It might be deep listening or even a meditative feeling. Softer colors, flowing lines, and water represent the emotions, where a lot of this sensory information comes in.

The brain takes in billions of bits of information every second, but most of this information is not stored in the conscious area of the brain. We can't remember everything! This lesson is really about developing the part of the self that is in touch with the subconscious and the emotional being.

Many symbols can be used to represent things hidden or what's going on below the surface. For instance, images of sailing or different ways of describing a reflection. (You can contrast these things with sharp angles and harsh lighting, as Orson Welles did in *Citizen Kane*). Dialogue that uses words to evoke calmness will work here. Pauses are important for this lesson. The character should pause to think or to feel, as if trying to get in touch with that part of himself that will let him know how he feels about what's happening. A lot of that will come out in the subtext as well.

In contrast, surrounding characters might make quick or harsh judgments and use dialogue that is snappy, intellectual, or sharp. Overall they may demonstrate the downplaying and almost ridiculing of empathy, intuition, and instinct.

The setting that you choose can evoke a lot of feeling and emotion. Consider which settings in the location that you are developing can reveal that introspection the character is trying to attain, and also the instinct, gentleness, gracefulness, and generosity. You want a place that is heart-centered and caring and also something that is beautiful.

The love interest can be very intuitive or not intuitive at all. There could be a situation where the love interest is not speaking her mind about how she feels about the relationship, and the hero is trying to read her but can't. This could make an appropriate subplot. The hero is inspired to use instinct and intuition to understand what the woman he's in love with is trying to express.

These skills might also be used to know an elusive villain. Often in crime shows, the officers have to be intuitive, depending on the type of villain they are dealing with. The villain's behavior can be so erratic. If pieces of the crime puzzle don't fit together, the police don't know what they are dealing with.

They turn to the criminal's psychological profile and see what they can find out about him. In the process, they have to go with their gut. They try to and interpret certain things that the villain has said and what those things might mean. They have to guess what the subtext behind his actions might be. Such tasks require using their intuitive sides quite a bit. In a detective's story, you will come upon this quality quite often.

TWISTS

For a twist try a gender reversal. Feeling and intuition, gentleness and innocence are traditionally attributed to women and children. One twist might be to portray a woman who lacks all of these qualities and the characters around her see her as flawed.

AUDIENCE INTEREST

An audience might think it's silly for the character to try to use intuition. They may expect the character to fail (unless your story is about psychics). The public doesn't generally accept that all people have an innate ability to be intuitive. But attitudes are changing.

Innocence, living in the present moment, and being sensitive and observant are not valued ideals in American society. Yet, deep down, some of us wish we were these things. We want to keep our innocence and to have fun and not worry about safety or someone trying to take advantage of us. But we also see intuition as a gift only few can master. We want intuition to work for us, but we categorize it alongside magical power.

CHAPTER 12

THE DOLPHIN

TRANSCENDENCE, HARMONY & PURPOSE

"Dolphins teach us how to play and open up to joyful experiences in our daily lives. Dolphins often appear when a person is swallowed up with their work as a reminder that everyone needs to take a day off now and again to play. They also teach love of self. Blow-out your blowhole and breathe in some new life. You'll feel better." —Phylameana Desy

I've had many interactions with dolphins recently, and they have been quite amazing. My time on a dolphin safari was especially memorable. I was in a boat surrounded by hundreds of dolphins, including babies. They are so playful and beautiful to see in their wild habitat. I petted a dolphin at Sea World once, and it too was a wonderful experience, but not as great as seeing these great creatures in their own environment, enjoying life in a pod.

Dolphins can never fall asleep completely. Half of a dolphin's brain has to be working at all times so the dolphin continues to breathe. One half of the dolphin's brain will go into a delta sleep state, while the other half remains awake. This delta sleep state is considered the highest level of consciousness, which great masters try to obtain through meditation

The dolphin's lesson is to transcend, harmonize, and find purpose in life. Dolphins create groups and communicate in such a way that whatever one dolphin sees, they all see. A sense of individuality is important, too, but they are so connected as a group and care so deeply about each other that they exist in a state of constant communication. I'm not sure if such a thing occurs in other animal groups. Dolphins constantly walk two worlds at once—they have two halves to their brain, which can think individually, and they need both to live in water and breathe air to survive.

As symbols, dolphins teach about becoming a more enlightened person, who reaches his full potential. In this case, full potential means the highest level one can aspire to (especially on a spiritual level). That's the biggest part of the lesson of the dolphin.

THE DOLPHIN'S CHARACTER ARC

In this arc, the hero is learning to be the absolute best, at the top of his game, in some area of his life. Striving to be the best is the focus of the plot. The story might be based on the development of a skill, it might be based on striving to break a record, and it might be about reaching the peak of spiritual enlightenment.

An example is a story about a baseball player who wants to transcend what other players have done before by hitting sixty home runs in one season.

The dolphin is at the highest level which is really a natural ability and a natural state that we have forgotten. We put all these masks on and all the ego stuff that separates us and makes us operate or think we are much less than we are. So this lesson is not only about this character practicing in order to achieve some goal, but about his becoming more of who he naturally is by developing his talents and instincts.

You might have a character who is pressured to play soccer. He is practicing, practicing, practicing, and trying to develop his skills, trying to be the best player he can be, but it's still not happening for him. On the other hand, if he concentrates on his natural ability to play the violin, he very quickly becomes one of the best violin players in the world. This is because playing violin comes naturally to him. It is his true nature and he can reach the top of his "game."

STORY EXAMPLES

Story of an Hour by Kate Chopin
A woman learns of her husband's death and is at first upset. Then she feels unimaginable joy as she realizes she is free to pursue her interests. But the joy is short-lived (society will not stand for it as this story takes place a long time ago, when women were considered possessions) with a surprise ending. *"Knowing that Mrs. Mallard was afflicted with a heart trouble, great care was taken to break to her as gently as possible the news of her husband's death."*

Walden by Henry David Thoreau
Thoreau calls us to lead simpler lives balancing solitude and growth, and shows us that nature can support us in this quest.

2001: A Space Odyssey
An exploration of what it means to be human, and to discover how we came to be and whether we can transcend or not.

Siddhartha by Hermann Hesse
Addresses the spiritual journey of man and the goal of transcendence as Siddhartha embarks on a journey of his own making to find enlightenment.

Cool Runnings
A group of athletes from Jamaica try to race bobsleds in the Olympics. It is their calling and they go through many trials to try and fulfill it. After all, there is no snow in Jamaica and the odds are against them. They try

to be like everyone else, but they are not successful until they do things their own way and honor their gifts.

WHY MIGHT YOUR CHARACTER RESIST THIS LESSON?

The character tries to please somebody else—perhaps her father—by pursuing what she knows is the wrong path. Or maybe she is afraid of success because a lot of issues come with achieving at the highest level. She thinks, "*What comes next? What will people think of me? Will I have to leave my friends behind? I can't accomplish more than my parents.*" Ultimately she should realize the journey is important, not the destination.

HOW DO OTHER CHARACTERS VIEW THIS LESSON?

Other characters may have mixed feelings about this lesson. They may be wondering why the ability comes so easily to the heroine. They may not realize the heroine is simply going with who she is. The other characters also may take her lead and try to find their own natural abilities with which they can reach their highest levels.

It takes a special skill just to be able to see where your own talent lies. It may take some effort for the characters to discover what their natural abilities are and to figure out who they really are. The decision to go with their birthright is part of the process. In learning to be in harmony with themselves and fair with themselves as far as not downplaying his gifts, not downplaying what he can do and not giving it up for the sake of someone else's ego or opinions.

The heroine knows that to take the risk of perusing her talent may mean that she loses friends. It may mean changing her entire life. But she knows deep down that she has to follow her passion. Her passion will lead her to a life of joy, playfulness, and harmony.

SUCCESSFUL RESOLUTION

In a successful resolution the hero discovers her natural ability. Sometimes when people of a minority race are held down, people of that race try to change who they are to become more like the more dominant race. They should instead learn to accept and love who they are and reach the highest level they can regardless of culture or race. This may be easier said than done which would elevate it to the level of plot taking up more space in the story than just the theme or message but we commonly see this theme in such stories.

TRAGIC RESOLUTION

An unsuccessful outcome occurs when the hero can't open up enough to embrace his natural talent. The character allows other people to stop him from reaching the highest level. He doesn't respect himself, or he doesn't respect his skill and talent, and he is embarrassed about who he is. For these reason, he decides to stay where he is. Or if he does decide to go with his talent, he does not go as far as he needs to go to reach the highest level.

Someone of authority might keep him from getting the recognition he deserves. An example is a boxer who technically wins a fight, but because of the crazy point system, he is not awarded the win in the end.

HOW CAN YOU ILLUSTRATE THIS LESSON?

You can use symbols that portray:

- Accomplishing something
- Getting to the highest level
- Climbing a mountain
- Walking a straight path without being tempted into other things
- Being focused
- Working in harmony within a group
- Images of resurrection and rebirth
- Being true to oneself with joy and playfulness

The mood, tones, setting, and props can all promote a positive, open expanded feeling. They also might juxtapose such a feeling by promoting the opposite .

Images of teams are appropriate for this lesson. What group might your hero be a part of when he decides to pursue his natural talent and skill? Perhaps the team wears a uniform. You can use a lot of that imagery in setting and costuming.

TWISTS

Gender may be an issue with this lesson because a lot of things are considered unacceptable for women to do. If a woman's purpose in life is to do something society believes is unacceptable, you have a character in direct conflict with society rules. Think of Chopin's *Story of an Hour*. When the main character hears that her husband is dead, she is upset but then begins to see how much freedom she now has to pursue her interests as a widow she can do more and does not *have* to get married again. She feels unimaginable joy, until the surprise ending.

A twist can also play in culture and geography. Remember the bobsled racers from Jamaica? Where are they going to practice? The geography of their home proved to be a problem, but they still listened to their calling and did whatever they had to do to learn their craft so they could compete in the Olympics. It wasn't until they developed their own style that they became successful. They had to give up trying to be like everyone else.

AUDIENCE INTEREST

People like to see characters reach the highest level of mastery in their field. But we want to see them do it only after facing a lot of hardship. Since this lesson applies to heroes such as Beethoven or Mozart, who are really good at what they do, this makes for a problem. Their talent comes easily so their hardship will probably come from an element of angst and inner suffering—perhaps, the tortured artist syndrome. It also may come from other character issues, like mental and emotional issues and events from the past that come in and threaten to sway the character in the direction of self-sabotage. Talent will win out, especially if surrounding characters enjoy what the hero can do and won't want him to give up.

We find these stories interesting because the character's talent comes so easily, but other parts of his life suffer and are pushed aside because the hero finds so much passion in what he is doing. Just as he reaches the highest level of talent, the other areas of life fall apart. We enjoy watching the character deal with those conflicts. Everyone is looking for their purpose in life, so an audience will definitely relate.

CHAPTER 13

THE FOX

CLEVERNESS & RESOURCEFULNESS

"The Fox's ability to meld into one's surroundings and be un-
noticed is a powerful gift when one is observing the activities
of others. This allows it to be the protector of the family unit."
—Sandy Pounce

Much truth lies within the expression "clever like a fox." Foxes are known to be able to hide very well by camouflaging themselves and can adapt to any kind of situation in a very clever way. Most animals run in a straight line when chased by a predator. But when a predator chases a fox, the fox will decide (when the moment feels right) to double back on its trail and run in circles. Doing so makes it very difficult for the predator to determine which direction the fox went. It will seem like the trail just ends and disappears. Then the fox can hide very easily to confuse the predator.

The fox is resourceful and clever. He is prone to thinking and behaving differently, and he approaches difficult situations from a perspective that doesn't occur to most others. The Fox's unexpected action might be shocking, or even seemingly stupid, but it usually works out.

THE FOX'S CHARACTER ARC

The hero finds himself in a situation where the outcome is pretty certain. The reader thinks she knows what's going to happen—there isn't much hope for the hero—but then the hero does something completely unexpected and turns everything around.

This kind of thing takes a lot of belief in yourself. Having some experience with doing things differently, so that you know it can be done, helps. A good example is Steve Jobs and his Think Different campaign for the Apple computer. The campaign appealed to a lot of people who wanted to be different and to think differently and to approach challenges in a different way. It's not necessarily about being a genius. It's about being clever and having a creative mind-set. Put simply, it's looking at a situation and finding a completely different way to deal with it.

It could be a case of health. If the doctor says, *"I'm sorry, but you have six months left to live and there really isn't anything else that can be done,"* then it's about looking outside the box and saying, *"Well, I don't accept that. There must be something I can try."* Perhaps you will go on a journey to try to heal another way. It's about finding inventive ideas and ways to solve your problem, whatever the problem is.

For example, my dad was a carpenter who did a lot of work on people's houses.

When the tools he had didn't fit together to get a job done, he would take a moment and go deep into his thoughts. He would find a creative solution to the problem by combining things no one ever thought to combine. And in that way he would get the job done on schedule.

Another example of this occurred with the recent oil spill in the Gulf. For several weeks, oil continued to gush deep under the water, and no one could figure out how to stop it. A simple plumber submitted some schematics online, showing how to create a fix that ended up solving the problem. That was inventive. However, the guy who said, *Let's put up a website so regular people can submit ideas, because we're running out of them*, was equally inventive.

When danger from a predator is involved, the fox is able to camouflage and hide very well. So this lesson also illustrates the element of cleverness in hiding. In a horror movie, for instance, the hero will use his clever thinking to hide from a crazy killer. In this way, he protects himself.

STORY EXAMPLES

The Hobbit by J.R.R. Tolkien
Bilbo confronts spiders, trolls, and the great dragon Smaug, all of which give him an opportunity to test his resourcefulness.

Apollo 13
Two days after launch, an oxygen tank explodes in a spaceship. The crew members must use their resourcefulness and quick thinking to make it back home alive using hoses, cardboard, plastic bags, and canisters

The Odyssey by Homer
In this epic poem, Odysseus's most distinguishing traits are his intellect and quick wit. When he struggles with the Cyclops, he devises a plan to use the Cyclops' strength to his advantage. He defeats the Cyclops and a boulder is removed from an entrance he needs to pass through.

Misery by Stephen King
A former nurse with an obsession kidnaps and tends to her favorite author after he survives a car accident. The author character tricks the nurse by asking her for a cigarette and match, lighting his new manuscript on fire, and then attacking her when she is distracted.

WHY MIGHT YOUR HERO RESIST THIS LESSON?
In many ways, the hero is taking a chance. Trying a new idea requires him to take a big leap of faith. If there are people helping him, he will have to trust them too. If lives are on the line, he'll feel the pressure. So it's a lesson in believing in himself and trusting a higher power as well.

HOW DO OTHER CHARACTERS VIEW THIS LESSON?

Supporting characters may be negative about the hero pursuing this lesson because he is trying something new and different. No one knows if his idea will work and some characters might want to be the voice of reason. If the hero ends up being wrong, then they can be right and not be held accountable for the negative consequences.

So they will automatically take the opposite side and have a fifty-fifty chance of getting praised for taking a stand. The hero will be praised if he's successful, and some characters will be jealous of his clever idea and bravery to carry it through. They wish they were able to come up with ideas like that.

Specific skills the hero might need to work on include being observant, being creative, brainstorming ideas, and finding a connection between different objects. The hero can study different art forms and different philosophers and ideas. He should be open to new concepts and the possibilities of how two things can be combined to create a third thing. The hero must have the skill to stop and observe quickly because usually he'll be under strict time constraints.

SUCCESSFUL RESOLUTION

A successful outcome occurs when a situation arises and the hero's clever idea and belief in himself solve the problem. He inspires those who are trying to help him and his idea is successful in saving the day.

TRAGIC RESOLUTION

An unsuccessful resolution occurs when the hero's idea doesn't work, or when he hesitates to act and somebody else comes to the rescue with a very similar idea and the rescuer reaps all the benefits and rewards. (An example is the competition between Bill Gates and Steve Jobs to create the first computer.) Or the hero fails to attempt his idea, and as a result a huge disaster occurs that could have been averted. As a consequence, the hero has to deal with a lot of guilt and shame. He wonders why he didn't believe in himself. A lot of internal agony may be associated with this lesson.

HOW CAN YOU ILLUSTRATE THIS LESSON?

You can use symbols of inventors and of inventiveness. Items that symbolize cleverness and a creative intelligence. You can have your hero make connections that are odd. An apple and an orange placed in a bowl can symbolize something like this. In the hero's home the decorations could seem a little off. His way of dressing might be a little odd. His friends may be eccentric.

You could have an unconventional character around to show inventive, clever thinking. The love interest could be exotic and flamboyant, or just the opposite.

The villain can be the predator that the hero is trying to get away from. The hero has no choice but to get clever and inventive because he can't go head to head with the villain for whatever reason. The villain might be some kind of natural disaster such as a tornado or flooding.

TWISTS

Some cultures don't support people who think outside of the box, so society might be a hindrance. There isn't much to do as far as twisting this lesson. The interest lies in how deep you can go into the cleverness. The twist comes from the outrageousness of the efforts to create new things. They may seem crazy and yet plausible at the same time. Such a story can be a fun challenge for a writer to piece together. It's a discovery and an invention all wrapped up in one.

AUDIENCE INTEREST

We enjoy watching people use their creative wits to get out of bad situations. For instance, the character MacGyver time and time again uses scientific prowess to save the day. The key is to make a clever solution plausible—it must seem possible or the audience will not root for the hero.

Keep in mind that the hero must use the materials he finds in his setting to put together a solution. Therefore, the setting is very important in this case. You must know the story's outcome in advance so you can go back and plant the objects and ideas the hero needs in order to work a clever way out. Make his solution feasible: The reader should remember having seen certain objects in the setting when they are used later on. This fosters reader participation, which makes the story more enjoyable.

CHAPTER 14

THE HORSE

FREEDOM & VICTORY

"No single animal has contributed more to the spread of civilization than the horse. Horse brings with it new journeys. It will teach you to ride into new directions to awaken and discover your own freedom and power." —Ted Andrews

This lesson deals with freedom, movement, travel, speed, and victory. Horses, despite their large size are prey animals, not predators. In my personal work with horses (horse whispering), I found that if I had a negative thought or really bad feeling, the horse would walk away from me. They are very sensitive to energy and intention, and they won't voluntarily be with you and follow you unless you are in a grounded, truthful state.

The horse could literally sense disharmony between my movements and emotional energy. (I'm sure you've been around someone who feels angry but says, "I'm fine," and fakes a smile.) Therapists use horses in therapy to help clients see when they are not facing a feeling head-on.

The horse also needs to feel free to make his own decisions about where to go and what to do. This gives him a sense of safety and comfort.

The lesson here is intricate. It teaches the heroine how to be free and to allow others to be free. It's about moving forward toward the goal, having access to speed and travel, and discovering the truthfulness that will lead to victory. The heroine must have a free spirit and she must intend to do good regardless of her goal. However, the horse is also about victory because those in history who rode horses succeeded in battle. But, as in *The Shawshank Redemption*, victory and freedom can be an inner experience.

THE HORSE'S CHARACTER ARC

The horse must learn to stop trying to control: He must stop trying to control other people, as well as the outcomes of events. He must also stop trying to dominate. He has in the past forced his will upon others. His character arc will take him to a place where he learns to work in harmony with others and he forms companionships that move forward in a way that instills freedom and truthfulness within himself and others.

As human beings, our fears, insecurities, and life histories cause us to grasp at things. We want to own things, we want to hold things, we want to control things, and we want to experience the sense of security that doing so creates.

However, in order to truly be free, we must let go. We must be truthful, relax, and move toward our goals in a state of allowing, not grasping or controlling or trying to dominate. We must allow the freedom of expression, relationship, and ideas to materialize in an organic way. The lesson is to be truthful with oneself about how one is feeling and what one wants to accomplish and why.

If the hero is clear about her goal and knows why she wants to obtain her goal, she can let go and allow the universe to help her. She won't need to control everything including her journey. Things will begin to fall in place for the character. Much like the horse who would not come near me when my thoughts were negative or when I tried to force it to follow me.

STORY EXAMPLES

Braveheart

William Wallace teaches the Scots, oppressed by the English that if they fight back, then though they may die in battle they'll never lose their freedom and dignity.

The Shawshank Redemption

Andy Dufresne is falsely imprisoned for life in the Shawshank Prison. Still, he finds freedom behind bars and helps others to become free in themselves.

Atlas Shrugged by Ayn Rand

The author, who believes altruism is incompatible with freedom, takes a controversial look at freedom. The world is crumbling under government interventions and regulations. The economy has ground to a halt. The "banker with a heart of gold" lent to borrowers on the basis of their need rather than their ability and went out of business.

WHY MIGHT YOUR HERO RESIST THIS LESSON?

This is a scary lesson to learn. Those who have a goal often have a vision of how they think that goal should proceed. We hold tightly to this vision, and sometimes we try to force things to happen. We dominate the vision until it materializes.

Obtaining something as planned gives us a sense of accomplishment and control over our lives. But often it doesn't work this way, and many of us don't achieve our bigger goals in life. What we need to do is let go and allow events to happen. When we let go, we create space for ideas and people to come in, and we allow our goals to come to fruition in their own time and space.

HOW DO OTHER CHARACTERS VIEW THIS LESSON?

The hero provides other characters with freedom. For them, the pressure is off. They are free to move about the world and do whatever they need to do. This can feel odd because they are not used to having true freedom.

At first other characters might be a little hesitant, wondering if the hero means what he says or if he has ulterior motives. Eventually they'll respect and enjoy the freedom the hero is attempting to give them, and they may be much more inclined to help and be involved in the hero's quest.

SUCCESSFUL RESOLUTION

A successful outcome occurs if the hero finds his truth. Things work out better for him when he lets go and, in the end, he receives help from others simply by giving them space. He successfully reaches his goal in a way he could not have imagined at the start of the story. The goal comes quickly because the momentum that comes from this can catapult the hero forward.

TRAGIC RESOLUTION

The unsuccessful resolution occurs when the hero attempts to let go—and does here and there—but ultimately can't resist grasping and controlling, especially when the goal comes within his reach. It's easy to revert to bad behavior when you get excited and you fear that what you want may slip away, so you rush in and try to control it. Staying in that free state where you simply allow things to happen is very difficult to do when you're standing so close to your goal. Also, when stress hits, we tend to revert to old ways of behaving.

HOW CAN YOU ILLUSTRATE THIS LESSON?

For this lesson, it may be something as simple as a scene in a restaurant. Your character decides to order something not on the menu. Or the character's significant other decides to order something not off the menu, and your character is alarmed: *"What are you doing? You can't do that!"* Such an exchange shows him trying to control his girlfriend's freedom and squashing her free spirit. Later he can encourage her by saying, *"Whatever you get, I'll get,"* to show how he has changed.

There are different ways to explore the idea of free spiritedness. It's not necessarily about hippies and free love. A free spirit can show up in the boardroom. It's an inner way of thinking. It's having spontaneity and seeing a curve when others see a straight line.

The dialogue can also be used to illustrate a lot about doing things differently or conversely of grasping, clawing, and obtaining. The lesson is about overcoming the desire to contain and control something.

TWISTS

There is no gender or cultural issue to play with here. You might show people in occupations typically considered very controlled and rigid acting more like free spirits. It is a very interesting lesson to learn about how you are, how you operate in the world, and how that affects the people around you.

The nature of this lesson makes for an interesting character-driven story. The energy this character puts out and how that energy affects everything in his life—his decisions, his choices, his thoughts, the friends, family, and helpers that he draws in or pushes away—drives the plot forward. The character must at all times be conscious of how he is behaving in order for him to reach his goal. (In *Braveheart*, for instance, William Wallace needed to inspire a lot of people and motivate them to risk their lives.) The hero needs to discover his free spirit and the freedom in his life in order to move forward. A lot of things may be keeping him from that freedom and therefore he is unable to move forward.

He's trying so hard to control everything that he won't listen to those who want to work with him and want to be there for him. This kind of energy can turn people off and push them away. Perhaps the story is about a family. A mom, who is so overbearing that she's pushing her kids away, learns how to allow the children the freedom they deserve and in turn brings the family back together.

AUDIENCE INTEREST

This lesson's audience appeal is very high. People have always been fascinated by horses, and a lot of the fascination has to do with the horse's free spirit and strength in letting go. Many think that if they act a certain way, they can control and harness the horse's free spirit and strength, but few understand the horse's energy. The only way to harness it is to give up control and invite freedom in.

CHAPTER 15

THE WHALE

NORMALCY & SELF-ACCEPTANCE

"As each family of whales has its own "song," you too can find your soul song to recall those memories stored deep in your super conscious mind ... Do not be guilty of wasting your own value, your own in-born strengths." MrKay.org

The whale is one of the largest creatures on earth, and its home is the ocean, which is enormous. So in many respects the whale is the perfect size for its environment. The whale teaches us to feel normal and okay with who we are regardless of disabilities or past circumstances or anything else that may set us apart. This may apply to a character who has been in jail or experienced an addiction problem or was born with a disability.

The whale's lesson is about finding the right environment and accepting yourself regardless of what others think. Some people may be more sensitive, meditative, or spiritual than others. They may see the world in a way that is different from how most others see it. Or they may be very inventive and simply need to find the right space and the right environment that will support them and let them grow.

It's about being with other people who have gone through a similar ordeal or who have the same issue (good or bad). It's about finding a place where you can flourish, once you accept yourself for who you are. The students who attend the mutant school in *X-men* are a good example.

This doesn't mean you should isolate your hero from different experiences, environments, and people. It means simply that a part of the hero's life should stand as a foundation for this unusual element, so that the hero can then go and do other things in a more holistic, balanced, and grounded way. This is especially important for the hero who has recovered from a past with addictions.

If the character tries to reject or deny this part of herself, her entire life will be thrown off balance because such radical self-denial feeds into a deep part of the psyche. It will be hard for the character to relate to and interact in other areas and other environments. Something else that's inherent to the whale is the depth of the water. The deep water relates to the character's depth of emotions.

Whales feel deeply, and their hearing is acute. Their sight is lacking, but to them poor sight is normal for the environment they are in. They are emotionally sensitive and have sensitive hearing.

Whales have a radical capacity for accepting things. For example, to them, there is no problem with their eyesight; it's simply not needed. It would be unlike whales to feel like they are less than other creatures. The hero learning the whale's lesson needs to accept whatever issue she is facing. She needs to find an environment in which she fits in so that she can not only blossom but deal with the emotional overwhelm that is most likely to come as she grows.

THE WHALE'S CHARACTER ARC

The character arc is a journey of radical self-acceptance. The heroine must do something outwardly that shows and supports who she is becoming inwardly.

You might have a person who, after much drama, accepts what is going on in her life and finally seeks help. Maybe she moves into a group home to learn how to manage life in general. Later the heroine can prove that she has changed by going out into the world, doing regular things, and acting in self-reliant ways. This only happens if she accepts herself. In order for her to do so, she must seek the training and the environment that will help her deal. From there, she can move forward in her life.

The heroine could wind up languishing in a small town where the natives are unfamiliar with what she is going through. Perhaps she ends up drinking or getting into destructive behaviors in order to suppress her true nature. For instance, maybe she is psychic and surrounded by people who think such things are 'of the devil.'

STORY EXAMPLES

The Muppet Movie
A young boy who feels different from everyone around him finds a TV show of Muppets and realizes he is just like them. His dream of visiting the Muppets in Hollywood comes true. He goes on a journey with the Muppets and along the way learns to like himself.

X-men
The X-men series is ultimately about being different in a society that can just as easily vilify differences as reward them. The X-men wind up creating their own community and school so they can feel normal and accepted in their own way.

The King's Speech
King George VI, who suffered a severe speech impediment, had to "man up" and become a good public speaker after his father died and his brother abdicated the throne. He pursued a cure and ended up embracing himself in this new role. *"Because I have a right to be heard. I have a voice!"*

WHY MIGHT YOUR HERO RESIST THIS LESSON?
The heroine must accept who she is and in so doing she must accept that she's vastly different from the people around her. This is a concept that

may scare her. As long as she holds on to her resistance, she can maintain the illusion that she is just like everybody else and everything is fine and she can go on thinking that maybe she can get rid of this small part of her.

She doesn't realize that if she would only incorporate her difference into her life, if she would simply accept it as a part of herself, then it would become a non-issue for her in the future. But she does not want to be different. She wants to fit in, to simply get along. She wants to be normal.

HOW DO OTHER CHARACTERS VIEW THIS LESSON?

Some supporting characters may wish to hold the heroine back. Others see that when she finally embraces her difference, she will move forward in her life and possibly leave them. They may feel jealous of the new environment she's moving into and the new group she is moving toward.

SUCCESSFUL RESOLUTION

A successful outcome occurs when the heroine recognizes her difference, accepts it, and allows herself to be a little different. Maybe she makes amends for being an addict by facing everyone she hurt. Maybe she pursues her talent for mixed martial arts fighting much to the chagrin of her mother and the other fighters. It doesn't matter if she wins or loses, it only matters that she accepts herself.

TRAGIC RESOLUTION

An unsuccessful outcome occurs when the heroine refuses to admit her difference, refuses to change, refuses to grow, refuses to accept this part of herself. This is a problem that will be very integral to who the heroine is, especially if she has addictions or if an incident in the past is haunting her and causing her to participate in destructive behavior that could lead to her demise.

HOW CAN YOU ILLUSTRATE THIS LESSON?

Blubber is a natural source of protection, insulation, and nourishment for the whale. You can surround your character with cocoonlike insulation. It can be a sort of coddling that other characters create around her to try to protect her or keep her in denial. What if the one who hurt the heroine was her own mother? The rest of the family may not want the heroine to uncover her past because it would mean dragging the family into a dramatic situation.

The heroine may be protecting herself from her own memories. The whole family may use alcohol or drugs, or may have other addictions (like watching too much television) to numb and insulate themselves. In many ways, the blubber for a whale is a positive thing, protection and nourishment. The heroine can find this protection and nourishment when she enters the right environment and gains the right skills. The heroine needs to make the move from the numbing way of dealing with her difference to the nourishing way of dealing with her difference.

In the setting this can show up symbolically. You can show how protective her home or world has become. Or you can show other characters trying to create a home that will protect this character from herself.

That sense of protection can come through in mood and tone as well. For instance you might use songs from the 1950s to illustrate society's view of life and things that your characters are expected to do on a daily basis. Random images and pictures that support the status quo will work too.

The subtext can be about doing what you are supposed to do and doing what is expected of you, being normal, fitting in, and toeing the line.

TWISTS

Maybe the thing that is so supposedly different about the hero is really no problem at all. Characters around the heroine can say, "*I just don't get why that was a problem. Everybody is like that; everybody has that and there really is nothing different about you.*" We often think we are the only one in the world who has a certain problem, only to discover the problem is quite common but we didn't know it until others shared their stories.

You might incorporate a twist where the problem actually exists in the character's mind. For instance, a character who keeps talking about having some really strange types of plastic surgery and the people around her don't get it. It is almost as if the heroine has body dysmorphic disorder where she sees problems that don't exist.

Your character may feel misunderstood because the rest of world thinks there is absolutely nothing wrong with them. She looks at herself and sees these things that are wrong, and she doesn't feel normal at all. She wants to change these things about herself in an effort to be normal, but because the problem doesn't actually exist there is nothing to change. This could be something the character needs to learn.

On the flip side, you can have a character who relishes being different and will do anything to remain so. She wants to be special. She wants to feel that she's better than everyone else. She doesn't want to heal anything and may have an inflated ego.

AUDIENCE INTEREST

Because we all feel silly or abnormal about ourselves in some way, we can all relate to this character and the lesson she must learn. We all have things in our past that we might be ashamed of.

This lesson will resonate more when a conflict is related to it, but even on a small scale, any character can struggle with something in their past or a perceived flaw in the present that makes them feel different. Audiences like to watch characters who are learning how to accept themselves and their differences.

Ultimately, the more comfortable you are with who you are, the more good you will attract in your life. It all starts with radical self-acceptance.

CHAPTER 16

THE WOLF

INDIVIDUALITY & THE GROUP DYNAMIC

"Even though living in close knit packs provide wolves with a strong sense of family, they are still able to maintain their individuality. Wolves represent the spirit of freedom, but they realize that having individual freedom requires having responsibilities."—Animaltotem.com

Wolves are very direct. What they say (grunts and growls) is congruent with their body language. They bump into each other, and they say what they mean. There is no way to misunderstand what a wolf is communicating. The group as a whole picks up on each individual's communication—no interpretation needed.

This is one of the best ways to work in a group. Learning how to communicate effectively is key to this lesson, and so the character arc teaches the value of being in a group and how to communicate to get things done when working with others.

CHARACTER ARC

The wolf is mainly about being able to work in a group to achieve a goal, or to survive. But at the same time, the wolves are able to retain their individuality within their social structure. Some cultures put an excessive emphasis on the individual and some put that emphasis on the group, but this lesson is about having both at the same time.

Learning how important the group as a whole is to individual survival and reaching a goal is key. A bunch of strong individuals coming together as a pack or a group can achieve many great things.

The wolf's lesson is about working in a group and accepting help from others in the group—a concept that a lot of strong-willed people have trouble understanding. Such types feel like they need to do everything themselves; nobody else can do a job as well as they can do it. Eventually they come around to seeing the benefits of belonging to a social structure—a family, a group of friends, people at work—that they can rely on. They see how this benefits the individual and how the individual benefits the group.

They also learn the good that comes with communication. Those who work in a group in any capacity must be able to communicate clearly, specifically, and directly. Humans tend to communicate in very incongruent ways; they might say the word *yes* while shaking their head no, and vice versa. Our body language doesn't coincide with what we are communicating verbally.

Many heroes try to go it alone, only to find they really need that sidekick or institution or a group. In *The Hangover,* the main characters mention their wolf pack. They vow not to tell anybody what happened in Vegas. And each guy expresses how valuable the group experience was to him. The wolf pack needn't be a lifelong group the hero will be a part of forever. It can take the form of a transient group dynamic.

STORY EXAMPLES

Their Eyes Were Watching God by Zora Neale Hurston

This story is about a heroine named Janie achieving a strong sense of self and finding her voice. Many characters try to stifle her and suppress her individuality but she learns to stand up for herself and use her voice (and sometimes silence) to her benefit.

The Crucible by Arthur Miller

In this story of the Salem witch trials, the author suggests that "there was no room in Salem for individuality," and uses characters John and Elizabeth Proctor to express this idea. They both voice opinions that go against authority and tradition, which is the essence of freethinking.

Avatar

Two groups of individuals work together amongst themselves but clearly one group (the Navi) is far superior to the other (the humans). The Navi includes nature and their home as part of their group and work in harmony to ensure a future in which all can prosper. The Navi rally to help one another and live by present moment wisdom over rigid rules, taking the 'individual' into account.

Little Miss Sunshine

A young girl wants to compete in a beauty pageant and the family has to learn to work together in order to make it happen.

WHY MIGHT YOUR HERO RESIST THIS LESSON?

In many stories, the hero wants to do things himself and thinks that sharing responsibility or asking for help is a sign of weakness.

So, the hero may resist having to learn this because he is living in a state of crisis or he wants the recognition for himself and going it alone will insure he gets full credit. He doesn't trust anybody else to handle the task at hand. It seems easier to handle it himself than to try to train other people and work with them when in the end there is no guarantee they'll get the job done.

HOW DO OTHER CHARACTERS VIEW THIS LESSON?

Other characters may want to be a part of reaching the goal so they are going to support it and try to work in a group and communicate well and help the hero get the job done. They also may have their own agendas and reasons for seeing the job is done. In other words, other characters might support the hero in reaching his goal but their reasons for doing so can vary.

Communicating well is a special skill. When instructions are not carried out well, it is often because the person who delegated instructions did not communicate clearly and effectively. It may take patience and an extra second or two to provide detailed directions, but then you can let go knowing the person doing the work understands what's expected of him. When working in a group, there is always a learning curve. In the beginning you just have to muddle through it. A lot of people have problems because they expect things to be perfect from the onset.

On the flip side, organizations that praise the group over the individual do not fully let their people explore their creativity. This is because often the group has rules and structures and systems in place for how things should be done. Therefore, the things an individual can offer a project often get lost. A lot of good ideas and opportunities may be lost when individual contributions are not being honored or sought.

SUCCESSFUL RESOLUTION

A successful outcome for this type of lesson occurs when the hero can remain a strong individual and contribute to the group and be able to communicate well and work well within the group to reach a common goal. He doesn't have to go it alone anymore. He doesn't have to stress himself out. He has seen the value of working in a group.

TRAGIC RESOLUTION

The hero tries to do everything on his own and fails miserably. It may be too late to allow others to come in and help him save the day. If he sees that he was wrong, then he has at least learned something in the process. Usually, though, he will go 'down with the ship' to prove himself right.

HOW CAN YOU ILLUSTRATE THIS LESSON?

You can illustrate this lesson with things that show communication. The characters can have body language that is congruent with what's being said, or not. In this way the lesson becomes part of the subtext.

The setting can significantly undermine a character. It can include images of the Lone Wolf, or things that are single. Or you can show items that typically belong in a group by themselves to represent the individual.

The dialogue can be very skewed one way or the other depending on the types of words that are chosen. People can speak in first person, with *I, me,* and *you* versus third person with *us, we,* and *them.* There are different ways of structuring the dialogue to bring out the idea of how the individual interacts with the group and the importance of communicating effectively. Perhaps a character mumbles or stutters.

TWISTS

The twist on this could be about getting into a group and learning how to communicate, and then butting up against another group. How does the hero manage that kind of dynamic? Does his group work with another group well? How do the two groups communicate? You can explore different types of groups and organizations based on different criteria, such as beliefs or religion, or whether they are charities, companies, or corporations. How do the groups interact, and how do the individuals from each group interact?

Or you could portray a group that does not communicate well but somehow fumbles through based on individual strengths. Somehow it still works.

A lot of stories address the issue of families and the individual who tries to leave the family. Perhaps the hero, having gone home for the holidays, finds himself back in the family setting again and the story is about how the hero fits back in—or doesn't. Very often it becomes about that person maintaining his individuality and not quite being a part of the family anymore.

AUDIENCE INTEREST

The wolf's lesson can be an interesting on for audiences to explore because depending upon one's culture the importance placed on the group dynamic can vary. Americans tend to live in an individual mind-set. In Asian countries the people share a more group-oriented mind-set. Neither side questions this much, but perhaps they should. Oprah once asked a family in India upon arrival there, "How do you live with your parents your whole life?" The father replied "How do you not?"

CHAPTER 17

THE EAGLE

DEEP RELATIONSHIPS & PATRIOTISM

"Eagle represents the deepest and most spiritually awakened
form of relationships, often requiring the complete surrender
of a previously held way of life or attitude. In essence Eagle
medicine relates to right relationship—relationship with self,
god, partners, nature, society..." —Askaura.com

Everything about an eagle is set up for a specific purpose. The talons, the beak, the eyes, and the feathers all have very distinct purposes in helping the eagle survive. The talons serve the purpose of killing prey, and the shape of the beak is set up to tear apart, eat, and consume the prey.

The eagle is interesting because it teaches the lesson of creating deep relationships and of having clarity; and then it also is the skewed symbol for political freedom (the all-American hero), which appears quite a bit in action movies.

Eagles mate for life in a dazzling and dangerous spectacle of soaring to great heights then free-falling, as a pair, over and over again. The lesson is in learning how to develop true intimacy and relationship with others—to take the plunge.

As human beings, the biggest risk we take in life is opening up to love and allowing others inside our hearts. Many of us get married but never fully open to love. Many of us are religious but never fully open to the divine. A vulnerability must be faced in order to be worthy of gifts of love. It's like stripping away our feathers and talons, and being exposed for a time.

There can be barriers to this:

- Other people can enable us to live at a distance.
- Our past trauma can compel us to do so.
- Self-centeredness can stop us from connecting to someone else.
- Without a role model, a lack of examples can leave us devoid of skills or knowledge to develop this essential part of life.

THE EAGLE'S CHARACTER ARC

The degree to which the hero fails at love is the degree to which he is closed off. Sometimes when a person is closed off, he clings and acts needy. Such behavior reeks of desperation and ends up pushing others away. Then the hero may become angry and demanding. The hero needs to be clear about his motives for entering a relationship (with a person, group, or spiritual cause) and know what it is he truly desires. He needs to make sure he is ready to make such a connection, that "his feathers and talons" are ready for the deep relationship he seeks whether it's in marriage, family, friendship, spirituality, or his career.

As the all-American hero: It's as if everyone is in love with the hero. He can do no wrong. He is at the top of his game and has all of the skills and tools that he needs to accomplish his goals. He keeps his goal in sight and may not experience much of an arc because the lesson itself becomes a symbol. The arc is simply the hero maintaining this image and handling the responsibility of it, while sustaining the skills and the tools needed to accomplish the goal. The hero starts out with skills, knowledge, and resources already at his disposal—he just has to step up. He is the ideal that we all aspire to, and he is not allowed to have flaws or fail.

STORY EXAMPLES

The Kite Runner by Khaled Hosseini

Amir and Hassan have a best friend relationship that is one-sided. Hassan expresses brotherly love for Amir, but because of class differences, true friendship is not possible. Amir and his father Baba have a difficult relationship. Baba, wants to control what Amir is passionate about and what he should do in life, and Amir feels he's never good enough. In Afghanistan, the characters live in different worlds, but when they move to America, without their servants to support them, they depend on each other. Other people (servants) enabled them to have a shallow relationship.

Wuthering Heights by Charlotte Bronte

One of the greatest love stories of all time, *Wuthering Heights* centers on the romantic relationships of several couples so as to explore numerous aspects of love and romance. It asks the big question of whether one can love another more than oneself.

WHY MIGHT YOUR HERO RESIST THIS LESSON?

It's scary to be vulnerable, and often a character doesn't know the first thing about how to relate to others. Social skills are not taught at school. Students simply fumble through them as they pass from kindergarten to high school. A lot can happen during those formative years that leads to an aversion to letting people into your life in a deep and meaningful way. The hero may have experienced many instances as a kid that scared him away from getting emotionally close to others. He may seem like he wants desperately to be close to someone, but then he sabotages himself without realizing he is to blame for his own situation. He has little clarity about this aspect of himself.

As the all-American hero, he might start out having the things he thinks he needs to accomplish his goal, but actually he does not want to face the fact that he may have lost his edge or some of his skills. This might be due to injury, circumstance, aging, or something that happened to a loved one. He's a little off his game in some ways, but he does not want to acknowledge it. He's not sure he can live up to the expectations that everyone has of him anymore.

HOW DO OTHER CHARACTERS VIEW THIS LESSON?

Other characters can become very jealous of someone finding real love and connection in this world. It's something we all aspire toward in life, a basic desire among all people. Misery loves company, however, and many feel if someone else has 'it,' that diminishes the supply of 'it' to be had. (Instead, they should see it as an example of what is possible.) Hopefully some characters see it as a sign that such connections are possible.

As all-American hero: Supporting characters are not going to be comfortable acknowledging that the hero may have lost his edge, unless, of course, they harbor jealousy and animosity toward him. Most will feel that somebody needs to be that symbol of hope and success and freedom. He's the go-to guy when they need to feel safe. They do not want to face the fact that he may not be the same guy he always was. This downgrading of strength or skill is a stage used in most action stories to create drama and call the hero into question. Will the hero save the day, or not?

SUCCESSFUL RESOLUTION

The successful resolution occurs when the hero is able to risk creating deeper connections and relationships in his life. The reward is a deep feeling of togetherness and a healing of the perpetual aloneness so many feel on a daily basis.

As the all-American hero, he's able to gather the tools he needs and he saves the day.

TRAGIC RESOLUTION

A tragic resolution occurs when the hero continues to sabotage himself and misses out on developing meaningful relationships in his life. He's not strong enough to risk vulnerability. He probably doesn't think he could survive a letdown. Something from his past still has a hold on him, and he can't find a way to heal and move on.

As the all-American hero, he would not acknowledge his shortcomings, which could manifest in his ability to inspire and motivate others to help him. The shortcoming need not be physical. It might be that he is not able to acknowledge whatever issue is keeping him off his game, and it winds up taking down the entire project or goal.

HOW CAN YOU ILLUSTRATE THIS LESSON?

Showing things in the setting and props that convey pairs, couples, love, depth of feeling, poetry, and connection. Other couples in various stages in their relationship can appear. A child may push him to open up and successfully break down his walls. Children and animals can do such things because they don't ask for much in return, whereas a love interest or group may ask for a big commitment of his time. True love is about the other instead of the self, and children and animals have a way of bringing this out naturally. Children are very honest, and pets can mirror our internal feelings and behaviors.

As the all-American hero: The workings of this lesson can show in the placement of a lot of different symbols and settings and costumes. You can include many things having to do with heroes—just the idea of what it is to be a hero and what it means to step up. You can have awards show up in the setting. For contrast you can have a character who does not have these things, or thinks the awards are a joke or ridiculous. Maybe he achieves things in other ways, sort of fumbling around because he does not have the hero's skills, but he is able to achieve some goals and helps to save the day.

We have seen stories where the hero is at the top of his game and everything is great, and then for some reason or another he loses faith. He cannot pick himself up to even try to reach the goal anymore, so other characters step in and bungle around and try to do the job for him though it doesn't help very much. In one way or another, however, their efforts eventually rally the hero to give it another go. Then the situation works itself out.

So other characters can inspire the hero in that way, and the dialogue can be very motivational, the mood and tone can be uplifting and very focused. After all, the eagle's lesson is about focusing and keeping a goal in sight.

On the other hand, when the hero is failing, you could portray things as out of focus and kind of fuzzy. Supporting characters are not sure what is going on with the hero. This can add to the tension of wanting to get the hero back on track.

TWISTS

The hero's love interest might be very different from what we expect. Maybe there is an age difference, or a cultural difference, or differences of beliefs.

As the all-American hero: Twists of age and gender work well here. Today's audiences are more diverse and are often interested in action heroes other than the typical man in his thirties saving the day with explosions and guns. Today's hero may have a range of unique skills which may be intellectual, creative, observation oriented, or communication oriented. Perhaps the hero is in a jungle somewhere and learning to communicate with a tribe in order to help them.

AUDIENCE INTEREST

Audiences are interested in seeing love relationships work out. They want to learn from what they see or read. Love is something we all strive for in life. We all want to experience a deep connection with another person.

As for all-American hero aspect of the eagle, audiences want to believe that someone out there is ready and willing to save the day. In real life, we rest easy knowing we can depend on police and firemen, if we should need them. We like that they are specially trained and always on their game. On the other hand, we also like stories in which those heroes are made more human so we can better relate to them. We want to know we can count on them but it makes a good story if they, too, have weaknesses they must overcome.

CHAPTER 18

THE HUMMINGBIRD

FINDING INNER PEACE

"Hummingbird—the tiniest of all birds—brings special messages for us. It is the only creature that can stop dead while traveling at full speed. It can hover, or can go forward, backward, up or down. It lives on nectar and searches for the sweetness of life. Its long tongue lets it bypass the often tough and bitter outer layer to find the hidden treasures underneath."—Crystallinks.org

The hummingbird symbolizes hope and joy, and seemingly has energy that comes out of nowhere. They never tire. Their wings move so fast that they are merely a blur. Many people can see the infinity sign when these birds flap their wings—that's how fast those wings flap.

Hummingbirds are endowed with a playful quality. Years ago, I had a sun deck that they would visit with the intention of just sort of looking at me. When they came, I sensed their joy and playfulness. They zipped around, doing their thing and looking so calm and happy. That is what the hummingbird's lesson is about: enjoying the moment to such an extent that you have utterly no concern for the past or future. People rush around a lot, not thinking, making mistakes, not being able to sit down and be quiet and find some peace.

The first time I saw a baby hummingbird I thought it was a large bee and I screamed. That was a lesson in perception and how one's view of things can change her experience of them.

The hummingbird also teaches to live the following Zen saying: *"Before enlightenment, chop wood and carry water. After enlightenment, chop wood and carry water."* Life itself does not change when we learn such lessons, but we live life in a more peaceful and whole way after they've been learned.

From life experience we know joy and sorrow are never far apart, so this is not to say that your character will experience total joy and sweetness through this whole lesson.

THE HUMMINGBIRD'S CHARACTER ARC

The hummingbird's lesson is one of learning how to be present in all moments of life in order to find the joy in it. Modern society does not teach how to do this, and often when people try to do it, all of their problems and stresses flood into their minds. It can be quite painful and anxiety producing. Just take a moment and try to meditate for a few minutes and see what happens.

A lot of characters can struggle with this concept. Busy moms who manage a lot of children are a good example. They sometimes need to lock themselves in the bathroom to get a minute of peace. Learning how to relax and see the life that is happening all around you is a great way to recharge and handle this boundless energy to do everything else that one needs to do throughout the day.

An example might be a serious businessman and his assistant, who has done everything she can to get him to take some time off, but it is not until he gets hurt and needs to recuperate and do nothing, that he finally learns the lesson. After he reevaluates his life and his priorities, he goes for what is really important. This kind of major overhaul can require a lot of stirring up. It could take a couple of days, a couple of weeks, or a couple of months of reorganizing things and being in even more chaos and more craziness as he takes the steps to change life.

The same kind of thing happens when a person realizes it's best to downsize—to move out of a huge house into a smaller home (or a condo) in order to save money and relinquish all the stress that keeping up with a huge mansion brings about. It's the kind of decision that produces several months of chaos and increased activity before the goal of the new home is achieved.

Difficulties often are dredged up in the process of making a change. If this lesson is the whole story, as it often is in the Chick-lit genre, the heroine gets some sort of wake-up call to change her life and move forward in a different way.

STORY EXAMPLES

Star Trek: Insurrection
In a scene with Jean-Luc Picard and Anij, one of the planet's inhabitants, Anij "freezes" time and tells Jean-Luc that he needs to slow down and find the joy in common moments. One of the quirks (benefits) of the natives of the planet is that they live a long, long time and some of them can learn to freeze time in order to longer enjoy a pleasurable moment.

The Bean Trees by Barbara Kingsolver
The heroine's growing respect of the land and the natural world—shown through her delight in seeing a first summer rain in the desert—reflects her growing understanding of Native American identity.

WHY MIGHT YOUR HERO RESIST THIS LESSON?
It could be that the hero's health or finances (or some other area of life) has been neglected and it's becoming a huge problem. Perhaps the spouse or kids are going to leave because they cannot stand the pace of their father's life, or vice versa. The hero may have many important balls in the

air, and he simply can't fathom taking a break: If the balls fall, someone else might step in and take his place.

Other characters would probably support the heroine in her learning of this lesson because they would like to see a change in their own lives. They would like to have more simplicity and fun in their lives—almost everybody would. When there's a problem in our life, we often look to other people and situations and things as the source, but very often the trouble lies within. The heroine must look inside herself to find her heart-centered direction in life again, and supporting characters can help her do that. Perhaps she should quit her job as an accountant and open the bakery she always wanted to own.

SUCCESSFUL RESOLUTION

A successful outcome occurs when the heroine experiences an internal shift and decisions are made that lead to a restructuring of her life and, in turn, a lot more joy and relaxation in her life. She may continue at the same job and live in the same environment, but she must be a different person on the inside so that her experience of life has changed.

TRAGIC RESOLUTION

An unsuccessful outcome occurs when nothing ultimately changes. The heroine does not want to rest or recuperate and she makes herself more and more unhappy. She does not heal and she is not changed in the end.

HOW CAN YOU ILLUSTRATE THIS LESSON?

You can show images that invoke peacefulness and meditation. Or you may display the opposite: chaotic messiness that does not offer a chance to relax—the chaos that needs to be ovecome. Perhaps there are no comfortable chairs to sit on, no place to read. Maybe televisions blare in every room and a host of distractions demand attention (a barking dog, a buzzing oven timer). In such a place, there is no opportunity to sit and be still.

You can create a color scheme, structure, and decor void of peace. The heroine can move from setting to setting, never finding an appropriate place to rest.

TWISTS

You could have a character who decides she likes the chaos. Some people really do like drama and craziness because they grew up with it and it's all they know. Some people are uncomfortable with peace and quiet—they crave the jolts of adrenalin an unstable environment provides.

People who take a lot of risks, such as skydiving, crave that feeling of rushing adrenalin. They have a lot of trouble sitting still. The twist might be that the heroine comes to the conclusion that there is nothing wrong with her, that she does not actually desire peace and quiet after all. She understands that she has a little too much drama in her life and it's not healthy, but the idea of peace and quiet and being present all the time is not necessarily what she wants after all. She makes the decision from a healthy place, so she knows it's the right one. And that could be the twist.

Whatever the outcome or decision is, the heroine experiences a renewed sense of energy and feeling okay with her life. She either achieves the peace and quiet or she discovers that she's okay with not being that way. She is comfortable and has achieved a sense of joy on her own terms.

AUDIENCE INTEREST

This lesson's audience appeal is high because so many people strive for peace and joy in their lives, but not many know how to achieve it. It is interesting to watch a character look outside of herself for answers and come to the realization that the changes need to be made internally. Will she do it? If so, how?

CHAPTER 19

THE TIGER

MYSTICISM & KINGSHIP

"Tiger stalks, the sheathed claws and defined muscles can transform in the space of a heartbeat from fluid, casual movement to a powerful burst of energy" —NamasteCafe

The tiger shares many qualities with other big cats including panthers and lions.

Being at the top of the food chain means they don't have to worry about surviving the wild. Their strength, beauty, power, and ability to survive allows them the freedom to create vast territories, and to lounge around and enjoy life. Their power goes unchallenged and their beauty is immense.

I once visited a large cat preserve in California (shambala.org), where I was literary ten inches away from tigers, lions, and panthers. A chain-linked fence stood between us. It was a mesmerizing experience to be that close to these animals and to feel their power staring back at me. It was clear to me that they could choose at any moment to harm or not. I felt their raw instinct and knew somehow that if they wanted to attack, there wouldn't be much I could do about it.

Yet something else drew me in as well. The cats displayed all of this power, yet I sensed something similar to typical human emotion. You would never see an animal like this abuse or torture a fellow friend, female, or offspring. It was just pure instinct.

THE TIGER'S CHARACTER ARC

The tiger's lesson is more conceptual in that it is an invitation into the mystical realm. It's about being kingly, but with some sensuality and unpredictability. It's about exploring big questions at a deep level. It is about examining life and why we are here, and thinking more deeply about how we live and the different systems that govern our lives. It's about learning how to use your power and position in a healthy way; that is, how to be a king, not a tyrant.

You must have your basic needs met before you can explore these deeper aspects of life. In this way, the Tiger is set.

The character arc for this lesson can be:

- The hero finds himself coming to a crossroads, coming to a place where everything he wanted and has accomplished, all of his earthly goals, are achieved. He may not have much of a goal left to pursue except for enlightenment. He could be on his way toward reaching his goal when he wonders, "What's this all for?" This lesson could impact the plot in a big way because he may decide to abandon the main goal of the story.

- Or, you've hit the midpoint of the story and the goal is achieved and the readers are wondering what's next. We know the story is going to continue, but there's a moment of wondering if the writer messed up. Then the hero does something to cause a new direction to emerge, a higher longing brings with it a new goal.

- Or, the hero is learning about the right use of power and how power can corrupt.

- Or, the hero is learning about mystical power and otherworldly knowledge.

Tiger is about adventure and being colorful and exploring the world and new ideas. You're at a place in life where the basic needs are met and you have the option to think about other things more deeply and explore the meaning of life and what it means to you.

Having some sense of honesty and wanting to find answers is key because sometimes people already have an agenda to prove. They will explore things, but they already have an answer in mind and they are trying to prove that answer. It's important for them to be open-minded about what they might find or what they're looking for and allow those answers to take them in different direction.

The hero can be somebody who retires early. Now he can do more of what he wants to do. The hero can be born into money, or he may inherit money, and it allows him to find a new purpose in life.

I lived in a building once with a lot of celebrities and people who had trust funds. I found it interesting to observe these people, who had lots of time and resources, and to see what they did with them. In some cases they were self-destructive because they were bored and couldn't find meaning in their lives. In others, they were more balanced. Someone taught them to be more charitable and to take interest in social good and making changes in life in general. Some friends of mine, for instance, started Mindshare—a community organization in downtown L.A.—to explore ideas, yoga, and technology.

STORY EXAMPLE

Macbeth **by William Shakespeare**
Macbeth is consumed with ambition and wants to become king but winds up becoming a tyrant instead, as he goes to great lengths to keep his title.

WHY MIGHT YOUR HERO RESIST THIS LESSON?
This lesson is not taught very often because few people have the opportunity to fully stand in their power and question everything in life. It's not

only about having an abundance of money, however, because plenty of people seeking this type of greater understanding live in communities, communes, and monasteries, where the basic responsibilities are shared and needs are met without their having to spend time earning money for a living. Though their needs are not met with money, these individuals are able to engage in activism and exploration. Still, living in such a community may be hard for the hero to embrace, especially if he has family or friends who oppose the idea.

HOW DO OTHER CHARACTERS VIEW THIS LESSON?

Other characters may not understand the hero's need to pursue this lifestyle. They may think it's frivolous because they don't have the option to do such things and therefore have not fully considered it. Other characters may be supportive if the situation involves some sort of charity or activism. Those are things people understand. A general questioning of life, however, most people are not as apt to understand.

SUCCESSFUL RESOLUTION

A successful outcome occurs when the hero is able to explore the big questions while keeping his foundation intact. He must also make a difference in his own life, in his own thinking and discovery and thus add color into his life, as well as unpredictability and adventure. Hopefully he changes in the lives of others for the better, as well as society as a whole.

TRAGIC RESOLUTION

A tragic outcome occurs when the hero is unable to step forward into this unpredictable exploration and positive use of power. He may be afraid of what he'll find, or he may be afraid to question his faith. That happens a lot in deeper mystical explorations.

HOW CAN YOU ILLUSTRATE THIS LESSON?

The hero may not fully jump into this new life and may wind up involved with alcohol or other vices that numb his boredom (he is not necessarily in pain). He needs to find something of greater purpose to pursue, something that will contribute to a feeling of being needed and valued. You can use symbols, subplots, subtexts, dialogue, and tone in ways that suggest mystery and questioning. In this case, darkness or the unknown, reflections, exploration, vibrancy, sensuality, and items that show the hero in the process of seeking are appropriate.

Be sure to include the details of where the character lives and how he dresses. Also, you must show him and his ability to attract the opposite sex into his life and find fulfillment in that vein. All of the ways his basic needs are taken care of, and that he is not lacking anything material, can be a big part of the setting, costuming, and props. The dialogue should be very profound in the places where he questions life.

TWISTS

Twists on this lesson can occur if the hero starts questioning life in a negative way, for instance, a way that pulls him down a path that isn't about mysticism or enlightenment. He gets wrapped up in something that is not working for the social good, though it may have started out that way. For instance, perhaps he becomes involved in a cult or in a revolution that is not helpful. He does not have the best intentions and instead is manipulating people or giving money to a cause that turns out to be harmful. Or maybe the money he donates is not being used for what the leaders of the cult say it's being used for. In that case, a deeper exploration of trust and ethics becomes part of the lesson.

AUDIENCE INTEREST

Audience appeal is high for this type of story because most people want to know what their purpose is and how they can leave a legacy. Most of us don't have the time to explore the big questions so we look for books that will do it for us. Unfortunately most of them fall short.

CHAPTER 20

THE SNAKE

TRANSFORMATION, DEATH & REBIRTH

"The snake dwells in so many places, climates and environments, comes in so many colors, shapes and sizes that this creature can be said to be one of the most versatile of all. Indeed snakes represent versatility, transmutation and change, their natural inclination to "shed their skins" leaving behind the old, and adapting to the new, supports this idea." —Zahir Karbani

In school, I had a friend who had an eight-foot snake for a pet. We were all in awe of it. I was able to touch it and wear it around my shoulders but I always had a feeling of fear when I did so. It was hard to connect with the snake. It didn't offer the friendliness you might find in a dog or cat or even a squirrel. The snake was more independent minded, flicking his tongue about, trying to figure out if you were friend or foe. I'll never forget the time my friend sat the snake down and pulled out a small animal to feed to it. I watched as a very primal scene took place that day.

My friend really loved that snake. His mom, on the other hand, brought out a kitchen knife whenever it was near. "Keep that thing away from me," she said. Snakes evoke fear because they are hard to control. They can hide themselves at a moment's notice, and what you can't see, you fear.

THE SNAKE'S CHARACTER ARC

This lesson is about letting go of your 'self'—of your identity as you know it. Just as the snake sheds its skin, the hero will go through a rebirth and transformation. The lesson includes an element of letting go and allowing something greater than yourself to pull you along. There is no stopping this type of transformation once it has begun.

During the course of this arc, a major change in conditions occurs or a creative awakening happens. Some see the snake as a devil and some see it as a transformer or a healer. If you fight the snake's efforts, it can feel like a devilish force has come into your life and disrupted everything. It is better to accept it as more of a process of healing or a positive opportunity. The character arc produces a sense of complete, almost traumatic, transformation.

The hero really doesn't have much of a choice in the situation. Something comes into the hero's life and demands the hero let go of everything and become completely reborn. As part of the transformation, the character may go away and hibernate the same way snakes disappear in colder months. So, not only do snakes shed their skin and go through a renewal process, they also disappear for a while to help foster this transformation.

Unusual elements may play a part as well. Just as snakes are known for smelling with their flickering tongues, the hero may have a special skill or talent that helps with his transformation.

STORY EXAMPLES

The Lord of the Rings **series by J.R.R. Tolkien**
Frodo does not ask for the ring or the responsibility he must bear, but it is thrust upon him and he must endure his task for the whole world is at

stake. Other characters try to help him but ultimately he must go it alone leaving his entire life behind.

The Fly
A brilliant but eccentric scientist begins to transform into a giant man/fly hybrid after one of his experiments goes horribly wrong.

Halloween
A psychotic murderer escapes his institution and stalks a bookish teenage girl and her friends while his doctor chases him through the streets. The girl goes through a harsh transformation as she learns about the darker side of life, fear, and survival. In the end, she is a completely changed person—in some ways for good and in some ways for bad.

WHY MIGHT YOUR HERO RESIST THIS LESSON
The kind of change the hero will have to endure means change to the hundredth power. Most people avoid change to begin with, and this kind of change is not usually pleasant at all. The hero will face some very intense stuff. It can be an inner trauma in which she faces personal issues or it can be a situation where outward events come at her. Either way, it is an extreme, traumatic event that is going to take place.

Most people resist this kind of change. If the character is very well balanced and has been through something like it before, it won't seem harsh at first. Many CIA agents who have been captured in the past may not think that being captured again is a huge deal. In anyone else's opinion, however, it is an extreme situation. The heroine can see it as a challenge or a transformation rather than a complete 'why me' pity episode, if she chooses to do so.

HOW DO OTHER CHARACTERS VIEW THIS LESSON?
The heroine's lesson may make supporting characters feel uncomfortable, because no one likes to go through drastic changes in life. We like to think that if we face our little pebbles (problems) along the way, we won't get hit with a big boulder. (This is usually true, but most of us ignore the pebbles.) Watching someone go through such a dilemma can be traumatic

in itself. Oftentimes people like to come up with reasons someone else is going through such a thing, so they can avoid that reason and feel safe.

For example, in the case of attacks and rapes, studies have shown that uninvolved people want to get as much detail as possible about what happened, especially about what the victim was doing. This way, they can find some way to place blame on the victim. Doing so allows them to feel safe, because they can rationalize that they would not do such a thing. In getting all the details, they are trying to prove that the victim wasn't just like everybody else and that this event could not have happened to just anyone, anywhere, at any time.

It is human nature to want to separate from this kind of experience and therefore the victim. This is how the other characters in this story may feel. An exception would be a Florence Nightingale kind of character, who wants to step in and help.

This is something that the heroine just has to endure and go through and come out on the other side of. Other characters can't do too much for her outside of helping her survive what she is going through (the equivalent of shedding her skin). During the process of shedding their skins, snakes can develop a film over their eyes, which impairs their sight and makes them more vulnerable. They depend on their sense of smell in this situation. Your heroine will not be herself during this time, and she will feel vulnerable.

SUCCESSFUL RESOLUTION

A successful resolution occurs when the hero is able to deal with her transformation, maybe even see it as an opportunity, and come out the other side a changed person for the better.

TRAGIC RESOLUTION

A tragic outcome occurs when the heroine comes out on the other side but ultimately does not survive it. Or perhaps she hasn't learned much from the process and her situation becomes bad again. She needed to change who she was before the experience, but the experience was so traumatic and her reaction to the experience was so traumatic that when she comes through it, she is more damaged and more unable to cope than ever.

HOW CAN YOU ILLUSTRATE THIS LESSON?

You can show this lesson with symbols of snakes, circular snakelike symbols, and things that are dark. You might convey a dark mood, dark tone, dark opinions, and a dark view of things. Loneliness, going away, and absence may work into the plot.

You can have characters that have been through similar situations and act as oracles for the hero. They might fill her in a bit on what is happening, what's going to happen, and show her the way a little.

Nobody can do this transformation for the hero, but guides along the way may help her understand things and they can symbolize what the hero is going through.

TWISTS

After going through the transformation, the heroine is blessed with knowledge, wisdom, riches, or something that she wants, at least inwardly, because she changed so much. So many people want this kind of blessing in their life, but they are not willing to go through the rigorous experience it calls for.

Another twist might be that other characters are actively trying to stop the heroine from going through this transformation. Often people don't want to see other people change because it calls attention to the fact that they themselves haven't changed. The hero would butt heads with these characters because she knows they are making it more difficult on her. She would need to get some space from them or resolve issues with them in order to continue on her journey.

AUDIENCE INTEREST

The audience's interest in this is almost voyeuristic in the same way that we rubber neck to look at car crashes. It's not that people enjoy seeing this kind of thing. They just can't look away. There is something about the possibility of death or coming into contact with death that captivates us. The snake's lesson is very much about that because the old self is actually dying and being replaced with something new.

CHAPTER 21

THE BUTTERFLY

JOYFUL TRANSFORMATION

"The butterfly is a colorful, delightful symbol of transition and growth. People with the butterfly totem are joyful people who appear to others as bright and cheerful...Butterflies teach us that change is positive and should be embraced. Butterflies are born after a period of struggle. Without the struggle the wings would not be strong enough to allow the butterfly to take wing." —Totemwisdom.com

I once sat at the beach and was visited by ladybugs and butterflies, a highly unusual occurrence for a beach in Los Angeles. The insects' beauty and peace in particular impressed me. They just floated along on the breeze, landing on my leg for a moment before playing in the air once again. They were so in 'flow.'

Unlike snakes, butterflies symbolize a more delicate transformation. They have a more divine quality to them. The hero's transformation here could be about moving toward a very positive outcome, such as a lifelong dream or love. Whatever it is, the hero wants to go through the transformation. A good example is the god Angus in search of his beloved after a lifetime of conquests: *"It was then that Angus saw he could never be with her in his human form. Only if he would transform with her, could he know her love fully."* There is something to gain and the hero wants to gain it.

Butterflies are sensitive, especially to the earth and the earth's energy. If something bad happens ecologically speaking, insects and butterflies are the first to leave an area. They are sensitive in that way. The hero might possess this kind of skill as well. He may have an awareness or sensitivity, or an inner knowing, that maybe he didn't have before or maybe he always had but didn't use.

THE BUTTERFLY'S CHARACTER ARC

This lesson brings about a total and complete transformation, more so than the snake does, because the butterfly begins life crawling on the ground and ends it flying in the air with beautiful wings. Everything about the butterfly has transformed in every way possible and those changes can be viewed from the outside. At the same time, it was a quiet change that occurred inside a comfortable cocoon that the butterfly built and willingly entered.

This is a transformation of joy and gentleness, and it is not traumatic. Instead, it is an example of divine grace, where something big happens but a lot of the work is done for the character. This is an experience that the hero chose to have and enter into. This can be seen a lot in spiritual areas of life where little things can be seen by the hero as the big hand of the divine helping him and then all of a sudden something happens that changes him for the better.

He can:

- Be healed
- Have his whole outlook changed
- Find a new path is laid out before him
- Be offered the help he needs
- Overhear a conversation about the exact information he need.

You want to be careful you don't use the 'hand of god' (known as *deus ex machina*) writing technique in which something completely implausible falls out of the sky to save the day. The hero must take an active role in pursuing something and helping to create the situations that allow for the divine assistance to come in.

The lesson is not something that's pushed on him per se. The butterfly creates its own cocoon and has a lot of control over the situation. So the transformation occurs when the hero allows nature to take over. Think of motherhood and the transformation that women's bodies go through and how their life is completely changed afterwards.

Joy, love, and gentleness are part of this kind of change. The hero can see how wonderful life after the change could be. It's a change that the hero wants to go through and does so willingly.

STORY EXAMPLES

City of Angels
An angel falls in love with his charge and decides to fall from grace to become human and be with her.

Sixteen Candles
The heroine goes through a life-changing birthday when she tries to figure out what to do about her crush on the most popular boy in school, while dealing with a multitude of situations beyond her control including her sister's wedding, a house full of extended family, and advances from the geekiest boy in school. In the end she is completely transformed.

Taming of the Shrew by William Shakespeare
Transformation is the most important theme of this story about changing someone into society's image. "*O monstrous beast! how like a swine he lies! Grim death, how foul and loathsome is thine image! Sirs, I will practise on this drunken man. (Induction.1.4)*"

Pygmalion by George Bernard Shaw
A Victorian dialect expert bets that he can teach a lower-class girl to speak proper English and pass her off as a lady.

WHY MIGHT YOUR HERO RESIST THIS LESSON?

A character might resist this lesson because he may not feel deserving of such goodness in his life of some reason. He also may not understand exactly what's happening. In the beginning stages he may feel very much like he is losing his identity and everything about who he is. If humans went through what the butterfly goes though in order to mature, the transformation of being born as an adult would be extremely intense.

In the beginning, when the hero is facing what will happen, he may feel unworthy or afraid of the unknown. There is no trauma, nothing is pushing him to do this, but he experiences fear of the unknown.

HOW DO OTHER CHARACTERS VIEW THIS LESSON?

Other characters are usually okay with what the hero is going through. It's a change, but it's a change that the hero wants to pursue. It may even happen without much drama. Sometimes a challenge sparks the events.

The lesson doesn't inspire the people around the hero to take action, but it can bring up issues concerning their confidence in him. They might see it as just another silly thing that he is trying to do. They may not support him or fight him. They also may not be very confident in him or what he is trying to do. They may not see the outcome that he expects. They can't see the bigger picture because they are not involved.

SUCCESSFUL RESOLUTION

A successful outcome occurs when the hero is able to go through the change and come out on the other side. He gets into the flow and goes for the ride. His mind is open to recognizing the events that are taking place—events that may be subtle.

TRAGIC RESOLUTION

An unsuccessful outcome occurs when the hero lets other characters put him down or take away his confidence. He stops pushing himself and doesn't go for what he wants. He feels like he can't do it. Or maybe he attempts to go through it and he comes out of it and something happens, but he has not quite achieved the goal and won't try again.

HOW CAN YOU ILLUSTRATE THIS LESSON?

You can show this by using symbols of feathers and fluttering things that symbolize air. Images of change, of going with the flow, going with the currents whether they be wind or water all produce an appropriate effect. Cleansing works here as well. As a symbol you might depict laundry hung up on a line with sheets blowing in the breeze. There are many ways to show transformation using air: going where the wind takes you, riding the currents of air, merging with nature in these ways. Consider the mood of the colors you present. The sky works well in this lesson because the hero is ascending to a more divine space, a higher space. Images of light, sunlight, the beach, and places that are open and inviting are also appropriate. Consider using sunflowers and objects that are hopeful. The dialogue can include subjects about looking forward or having optimism.

TWISTS

An interesting thing about butterflies is that they taste with their front legs. When they walk on flowers, they are actually tasting them. Doing so helps the butterfly pollinate the flowers. So the butterfly represents the skills of using the senses in different ways—perhaps using them for joy and almost a divine godly quality.

You could come up with unusual things for the character to pursue, as the writers did for *Little Miss Sunshine*. The little girl's big performance may not seem like a big deal to some, but to her, it was transformative. Being able to play around a little bit with the character and what she sees as a transformative joyful goal or outcome can be a way to put a twist on this.

AUDIENCE INTEREST

Audiences like to watch a character go for the goal. The hero here is driving and motivating himself because he wants to change. Even if someone else initially pushed him, at some point he gets on board with it. There is courage in that and sometimes there is a little bit of madness in it as well. It's interesting to watch the hero arrive at a thin line between courage and madness, and try to work it out.

INDEX